STOP! DROP! & WIGGLE!

7 Easy Steps to Happiness

STOP! DROP! & WIGGLE!

7 Easy Steps to Happiness

Gaia Shawna Morrissette

BALBOA.
PRESS
A DIVISION OF HAY HOUSE

Balboa Press books may be ordered through booksellers or by contacting:

Balboa Press
A Division of Hay House
1663 Liberty Drive
Bloomington, IN 47403
www.balboapress.com
1 (877) 407-4847

Because of the dynamic nature of the Internet, any web addresses or links contained in this book may have changed since publication and may no longer be valid. The views expressed in this work are solely those of the author and do not necessarily reflect the views of the publisher, and the publisher hereby disclaims any responsibility for them.

The author of this book does not dispense medical advice or prescribe the use of any technique as a form of treatment for physical, emotional, or medical problems without the advice of a physician, either directly or indirectly. The intent of the author is only to offer information of a general nature to help you in your quest for emotional and spiritual well-being. In the event you use any of the information in this book for yourself, which is your constitutional right, the author and the publisher assume no responsibility for your actions.

Any people depicted in stock imagery provided by Thinkstock are models, and such images are being used for illustrative purposes only.
Certain stock imagery © Thinkstock.

Printed in the United States of America.

ISBN: 978-1-4525-9512-2 (sc)
ISBN: 978-1-4525-9511-5 (hc)
ISBN: 978-1-4525-9510-8 (e)

Library of Congress Control Number: 2014905616

Balboa Press rev. date: 04/04/2014

Disclaimer

If you are just starting your healing journey from past sexual abuse or other past emotional or physical trauma Stop! Drop! & Wiggle! may not be a good fit at this time of your healing journey. You will need to spend more time experiencing, expressing and understanding your feelings and emotions that have been locked away. It is also important that you make sure you reach out and get professional emotional support from either a coach that specializes in trauma recovery like myself or a therapist or counsellor. You do not have to go through this alone.

Once you have created a support network and done the beginning stages of your trauma recovery then Stop! Drop! & Wiggle! will be a wonderful tool for you to have and use to reclaim your happiness.

The information in this book should not be used as a substitute for professional advice.

Acknowledgements

I would like to take this moment to give gratitude to all the awesome people that have supported me and helped make this book a reality.

I thank Sherry Andraza from the bottom of my heart. Without her tireless efforts of editing and adding proper punctuation this book would have been one very long sentence. LOL

Thank you Aileen and Dale my supportive Succulent Living Team of Awesomeness.

Thank you Francine Houston for your hours of support and cheer-leading through the sweat, tears and laughter while I wrote this book.

Thank you Sassy and Kim for opening up your house in the jungle of Costa Rica so Stop! Drop! & Wiggle! could be birthed with your Howler Monkeys.

Thank you to my cousins Kerrie and Leigh for bringing me to Prince Rupert, B.C. so that the beauty of the coast could inspire me to write this book.

I thank my incredible husband for always supporting me unconditionally.

Finally, I say thank you to all the people and experiences that have been a part of my life's journey. Without you this book would not have been possible.

Contents

Welcome

Welcome friend to **Stop! Drop! & Wiggle!: 7 Easy Steps to Happiness**.

My name is Gaia. I am the creator and author of Stop! Drop! & Wiggle!: 7 Easy Steps to Happiness and I will be your fabulous guide on this new adventure. I am so happy you have chosen this opportunity to join me and to gain the knowledge and understanding that will support your new life of happiness.

Before we get into the juicy details of how to fill your life with happiness I want to share with you some important information:

- There are a number of therapeutic concepts that I will refer to throughout the book, but don't fret! I will explain these concepts as I go. However, I have also included a handy section in Appendix A with a slightly deeper look at these concepts if you would like to learn more.

- Many of the chapters have a skill building exercise. Please complete these as you read through the book as they will help you practice Stop! Drop! & Wiggle! on a daily basis.

- I strongly encourage you to read the book through to the end before attempting Step 1. These steps are meant to be completed together in a holistic approach. I do not want you left facing unpleasant emotions without the tools to cope with them.

- Be kind to yourself. As you begin this adventure and start practicing your new awesome tools for happiness do not place judgments or expectations on yourself. It has taken you many years to master the art of suffering and misery!! So be patient, loving, forgiving and gentle with yourself.

- Once you discover you are 7 easy steps away from feeling happiness on a consistent basis you might panic. You might decide that it is too good to be true or that it will work for other people but not you! Maybe you will think there is no way I can do this! Deep down, you might even tell yourself the biggest whopper of all "I am not worthy of being happy!" I am here to tell you those, and all other reasons and excuses, are CRAP!

You can be Happy!

To deserve to be Happy!

You are worthy of Happiness!

Becoming Happy will not kill you!

You will be making amazing changes towards the new life you desire to live and express. Open your mind, body and emotions to create your new exciting possibilities. With just a little bit of vigilance, I truly believe you will learn to master **Stop! Drop! & Wiggle!: 7 Easy Steps to Happiness.**

Thank you for trusting me to guide you on this new adventure. I am excited for this opportunity to share the struggles and successes of my own journey into discovering and creating Stop! Drop! & Wiggle! and I'd like to make the following commitment to you:

I will always be honest, loving and forthcoming with you. My ultimate goal is to make your journey as fun and easy as possible.

Now, I ask that you make two commitments to yourself:

Don't worry. I've kept them easy for all you commitment phobic people.

- Read the book to the end.
- Then, practice Stop! Drop! & Wiggle! in your life for two full weeks.

Excellent!! Now, repeat after me!

- "I, [your name] commit to reading Stop! Drop! & Wiggle! cover to cover."
- "I, [your name] commit to practicing Stop! Drop! & Wiggle! tools in my life for at least two weeks to truly experience the benefits."

Way to go! Let the happiness adventure start today!!

 Good job! That wasn't so bad now. Was it?

Front Row Seat into Gaia's Mind

Before we go any further on this journey to happiness I felt it was important to tell you a bit about my history. About the struggles and challenges I have faced and how they have contributed to the most amazing and wonderful life I have now.

Let me warn you some of my story is sad and tragic and may even be upsetting or uncomfortable for some people. I share my story to inspire you and remind you that you too can create a life filled with happiness no matter who you are or where you come from! All you have to do is choose it in each moment of each day. So, please keep reading. This story has a happy ending. I promise!

 Here we go. Hold on to your hats!

Most of my childhood was filled with laughter, outdoor adventures, building tree houses, going on treasure hunts and catching frogs. However, the remainder of my young life was filled with severe sexual and ritual abuse.

Until I was seventeen, I had no recollection of my abuse. As a child, to survive, I had suppressed all memories of my trauma. As a result I was a very sad and angry teenage girl. I attempted to kill myself a couple of times but I had no idea why I hated myself so much. I just wanted to die and make the pain inside go away.

Sometime later, after I began therapy, I started to recognize the people in my life who had been, and still were, unhealthy for me. I made an important life change that removed these unhealthy influences and I started to build a life where I felt emotionally safe in my environment. At the time I did not recognize these people as my perpetrators nor did

I realize that this would be the catalyst that would allow my memories to surface.

This was a major turning point in my life and on some strange level it was a relief when I could finally begin to identify a reason for all the sadness, self-loathing and fear that I had been living with.

This began my long and winding road trip to emotional health. I needed healing on all levels; mind, body, spirit and sexuality. Over the years I have explored many different modalities and types of therapies including traditional talk therapy, movement therapy, energy therapy and play and art therapy.

My next significant life challenge began on my twenty-fifth birthday; I was seriously injured in a major car accident. My boyfriend of the time was driving and another vehicle ran a red light, ploughing into the driver side of our vehicle. The force of the impact was so great that our lovely van became wrapped around a tree. I suffered a head injury, broken ribs, nerve damage in my knee, whiplash and major physical trauma. I was bedridden for three months.

At the time I owned my own business teaching pottery and drumming. I was told by all the rehabilitation specialists that I would be in chronic pain for the rest of my life and I would most likely require heavy narcotic pain medication just to function. I would ultimately need to close my studio and give up my pottery and drumming.

I decided that was not going to happen!! I was not going to just give up my studio and my business. I was determined to find alternative pain management techniques. Good nutrition, swimming, massage and hot tub therapy became part of my ongoing wellness routine helping me to return to my former life.

However, this did not prevent the chronic pain cycles. If you have ever lived with chronic pain you will understand how difficult these cycles can be to break.

A typical pain cycle works something like this: during a moment of pain you might say to yourself "I am always in pain". Your brain internalizes this message creating more frequent and intense pain in your body building a self-perpetuating pattern of pain.

To complicate things further the pain associated with my injuries and the therapy necessary to heal my body created feelings of helplessness that would trigger memories of my former abuse. I would lose perspective of where and when I was and I would be immobilized by flashbacks. I needed a better way to manage the pain and break the cycles.

I discovered that by celebrating the moments when I was in little to no pain that I could create new thought patterns and my body would respond in kind. This is why I know with every cell of my being that the power of our thoughts and actions affect every part of our mind, body and spirit when we take control. We have the power to change our lives in any way we want.

Let's fast forward to year 2013. It was a rough and rocky road for me, but through perseverance and the help of my health team I am winning the battle. I'm no longer that scared little girl who's angry all the time. So here I am; I have spent the last two and a half months in the amazing jungle of Costa Rica outside a lovely little surfing village. All my bills are paid, my health is the best it has ever been since the car accident, I have zero debt and I am watching yet another epic, breathtaking sunset over the Pacific Ocean and all of a sudden I realize I AM SAD!

After overcoming all my life's struggles and challenges and I have everything I ever wanted; I am living my dream but I am not truly happy. It was in that moment I realized I was one of "those people"! I had been hiding behind masks and mantras but I was still filled with unhappiness and I realized that I had never truly been happy for an extended period of time and I FREAKED OUT!

NOOOOOOOOO!!!!!

I suddenly understood that I had been choosing to live a life of suffering and misery. I had been simply disguising my misery and chasing things I thought would bring me happiness. For example, I truly believed that I would be happy when my dream to live in the jungle finally came true. But here I was, living my dream and I was NOT happy!

CRAP!!!!!

This was the birth place of Stop! Drop! & Wiggle! I decided I would no longer be content feeling miserable, crabby or grumpy; it was simply unacceptable. But even with all the self-help experts and positive thinking gurus, the challenged remained. How was I to truly and sincerely change my thoughts and feelings without faking it?

I have experienced firsthand that our thoughts and feelings can shape our reality. This concept is commonly referred to as positive thinking or the laws of attraction. Therefore, happy, positive thoughts will create a happy, abundant life. Negative thoughts and feelings will create a miserable, crappy life.

So as the concept of Stop! Drop! & Wiggle! started to develop my goal was to help me truly change my unpleasant feelings into real, tangible, positive feelings. No longer the old way where I could gaily chant, "happy-happy, joy-joy" with a fake smile, while all I wanted to do was kick somebody in the shins.

You do not have to feel this way anymore either!

Now, as I face each of life's challenges I choose to learn and grow though happiness and not through suffering. I am able to fully enjoy the things I have in my life. I am a savvy business woman with a successful practice as a sexual wellness coach. I have an awesome, loving, sexy husband and we share a fabulous sex life. We live in a beautiful old Victorian home and I travel three months of the year exploring new and magical places. I have been white-water rafting, I have climbed a 50 foot waterfall and I have hiked a 5.4 km mountain trail. This has not been entirely without pain or challenges but these things no longer have the power to make me miserable. I am truly grateful for my wondrous life and it just keeps getting better every time I choose to be happy.

Are you ready to choose to be happy?

Why Do We Choose To Be Miserable?

I know, right now you are thinking, "WHAT?? I don't choose to be miserable". But it is surprisingly true; there are multiple factors that promote the miserable choice over the happy choice. In North America our childhood, society and even some religions help form our choices to be miserable. We are socially, emotionally, physically and spiritually supported if we are a victim, miserable or suffering. It's no wonder we choose to be miserable.

What do I mean by miserable? I mean angry, sad, frustrated, hurt, jealous, melancholy, afraid, just to name a few. These are all important emotions, but if we hold on to them, over time they can fester and become our default emotional expression.

Our default emotional expression is where we spend most of our emotional energy. It is the emotion that exists in the back of our mind as part of our subconscious. It is a part of our day to day lives when we are not even aware of our emotions such as when you are playing a video game, having a shower, driving your car or doing paperwork. If this is not a pleasant and calm state of mind life can really feel like it is hard and it sucks all the time.

Most of my life my emotional default was fear which contributed to all sorts of anxiety, stress and nervousness. My body was in a constant state of fight or flight response creating a lot of health issues for me.

During our lives-our childhood, early relationships, friendships, romantic relationships and even business relationship-we develop what is known as our core belief system. Core beliefs are the narratives that we tell ourselves that help define who we are and the world around us. The main themes are most often about love, trust, worthiness and safety. They are often created from personal experience or through observation of others; parents peers, teachers, cultural beliefs. These belief systems can be positive or negative in nature but we believe in them so strongly, so deeply, that we create experiences and tell ourselves stories to support them. As human beings we have a driving desire to be loved, safe and accepted and we will figure out how we need to behave in order to achieve that in our environment.

For many, we learn to choose misery as our default emotional expression during our early formative years. There are various factors in our childhood that can influence our choices later in life. It can be as simple as mild yet frequent disapproval from an authority figure or as painful as extreme trauma. From these early influences we can develop default emotional expressions where we choose to be generally happy all the time or we choose to be generally miserable all the time.

For example a child may find great happiness in building castles in the sand. In one swift stroke a bully can crush that happiness by smashing the castle. At this moment a child may learn that being happy is something that can be easily stolen away (core belief) and that it is not safe to express happiness and develop a persona that is always fearful or sad(default emotional expression). If you don't build the sandcastle then no one can destroy it.

 When I was a little girl the grown ups always seemed unhappy and miserable with only brief moments of laughter or joy. I learned that it was only OK to be happy for short periods of time or someone would come along and steal your happiness.

Here are some core beliefs a child may develop pertaining to happiness which can contribute to a negative emotional default:

- It's not safe to be happy.
- I am unworthy of happiness.
- If I become truly happy I might die.
- People will leave me if I am happy.
- As long as I am not happy no one can take that happiness away from me.

My old one was, "If I become happy I will cease to exist or spontaneously combust!

Once we develop our core beliefs and emotional default expression we often find support for our misery in our adult life through common social interactions. Let me illustrate.

You meet up with a friend and start chatting about what's been going on in your lives. How often has this common conversation drifted to include everything that has been going wrong in your life? Your friend will listen to you, console you, sympathize with you and support you in your misery. In turn you will likely do the same thing for your friend as you both continue to pour out your negative stories.

You are not alone. Does the phrase "bitch session" ring any bells? Almost everyone in our North American culture does it. Even me!

Then, after this emotionally charged outpouring you may say, "Oh, I feel so much better now". Or you may feel like you have bonded or become closer friends during that exchange. But what is happening in the background is you are supporting each other's choice to be an emotional victim or martyr. Now maybe you don't know what I mean when I talk about being an emotional victim or martyr.

Being the emotional victim is about passing on the blame for your choice to be miserable; it is everyone else's fault, the universe is out to get me, why does this always happen to me. There is no way to become empowered in your life while you are blaming others for your emotions.

Being the martyr is about taking on all the blame and responsibility for suffering and not allowing or requiring others to own their part. This allows you to wear your emotional misery as part of your identity or to hold it against others as a form of manipulation and control. As long as misery defines who you are you cannot be happy or make new empowered changes in your live

The emotional support we receive is like a drug fix which temporarily makes you feel better. But when the high of the emotional support wears off you will seek the next fix. This reinforces your subconscious desire to share your misery.

These friendly "bitch sessions" are also reinforcing many different core beliefs such as:

- Life is hard and always a struggle.
- Being broken or a victim is the only way people will give me comfort and attention.
- My struggle is worse than yours, therefore I win. I need to win to feel good about myself.
- Sharing my negatively charged experiences is the only way to bond or deeply connect with other people.
- Negative experiences and drama create a story that people will listen to. When people listen to me I'm important.

 Those may sound pretty crazy but core beliefs don't have to make much sense or even be on a conscious level. So, if you don't see one on the list that applies to you that doesn't mean you don't have them.

Bitching vs. Sharing

There is an important difference between bitching (choosing to be miserable) and sharing factual events. If there is a strong emotional attachment and you are seeking to elicit an emotional or physical response from someone then YES, you are bitching and choosing to be miserable.

So, next time you start bitching about the negative things and events that have been going on in your life take a moment to observe what emotional or physical responses you are seeking or receiving from other people.

It was Feel the Fear and Do It Anyway® by Susan Jeffers, Ph.D. that held a real epiphany for me. One of the exercises in her book was to not complain or bitch for one whole week.

When I read this, it was 2008 and I was in the Amazon Jungle with about 20 people to talk to. I thought to myself, "No Problem! There's no drama here. I'm an easy going gal that always sees the glass as half full. I have wanted to be in the jungle ever since I discovered National Geographic as a child. I am as happy as a clam. I have NOTHING to complain about."

Boy was I delusional! I didn't even make it half a day!!

So at the time, I convinced myself it was just a stupid exercise that was impossible to accomplish and I decided to work on healing other stuff in my life. But it wasn't just a stupid exercise! With the memory of Dr. Jeffer's book in the back of my mind, I gradually became more and more aware of my own social interactions and the emotional and physical responses that I had been seeking.

In 2011 I decided to reread Feel the Fear and Do It Anyway® and this time I was committed to completing this exercise! So every day, over the following six weeks I would wake up and tell myself, "Today I will NOT complain or bitch." I finally made it to four whole days in a row and I could not believe how hard it was. That's when I realized that I was choosing to be miserable!

In my opinion Feel the Fear and Do It Anyway® is a must read book! I encourage you to pick up the book and try the exercise yourself. I've included it in the Resources section.

One other area of our lives where we can develop deep rooted core beliefs is through religion. I believe that the foundation of all religious and spiritual beliefs is meant to be love, kindness and making the world around us a better place for everyone. However, some of the religious ideologies in our society teach us that suffering in this lifetime will be rewarded in the afterlife. Take a moment as a non-judgemental, external observer to look at your religious core beliefs. Do they support a happy emotional default? If not, it is my belief that you can be more influential and create deeper and more positive relationships in your life when you are happy and joyful throughout your day. You do not need to suffer to bring joy, peace, love and happiness to the world.

Being able to look at yourself through the eyes of a non-judgemental observer may allow you to gain new insight into your self, your thoughts, your actions and your emotions.

Repeat after me: This is a judgement-free zone!

So no matter how your default emotional expression of misery was created there is good news-you can un-create it. Woohoo! As we move through the following chapters I am going to show you how to start shifting your negative emotional default expression and reinforce a healthy and positive one. The importance of this chapter is to give you awareness and insight into how you got to this point. With this new found understanding you gain the ability to recognize when your emotional responses are being impacted by social influences and your negative core beliefs. With insight and awareness you gain the power to choose how you respond to your life vs. simply reacting to it.

This is super important:
DO NOT get stuck on the how and why!!! Focusing too much energy on your past will only serve as a means to self sabotage by keeping you attached to your misery. You need to just let it go and this book will give you the tools to do so.

"Let it go" is a phrase you might hear me say a few times throughout the book. I have often had people ask me, "What do you mean by let it go?" I created Stop! Drop! & Wiggle! to be a quick, easy way to move out of a place of suffering and misery and into a life of happiness but you still have to choose it. Letting go is about deciding that happiness is better than misery and then making the choice to do things differently; out with the old way and in with the new.

Trust me! It's worth it!

It is important to understand that I do feel compassion for any past suffering or trauma you have endured.
Your emotions and experiences are valid but it is time to stop giving the past so much power to control your present and future life. I want you to know you can learn how to control your present and build your future!
YOU DESERVE TO BE HAPPY!

What Do I Have to Gain?

Well, happiness of course!

Remember at the start of the book you committed to trying Stop! Drop! & Wiggle! for two weeks? The reasoning is that it will take time for you to change your default emotional expression from one of misery to one of happiness. Practicing Stop! Drop! & Wiggle! will have a long term effect on a subconscious level. The more you practice now, the less you will need it in the future.

 Remember that deep down even the crabbiest and unhappy person has an inner desire to be happy they just don't have the tools or they do not believe they are worthy of it.

So let's go on an adventure and explore the world of happiness together. I am going to ask you a few questions. Take a moment to consider the question for yourself before reading the following paragraph.

What is happiness?

Happiness is an emotion or feeling that has a wide range of expressions. There is contentment, happiness, excitement, joy, bliss, ecstasy.

What does happiness feel like?

Your chest may feel light and warm. Your whole body might feel tingly. You might become overwhelmed with joy and find yourself crying tears of happiness. You might feel like you want to give the world a hug or you may just feel content and know that in this moment everything is alright.

How can you express happiness?

You might smile more, laugh, sing, dance, skip, wiggle, whistle, giggle. You might express it verbally or by hugging or kissing others.

> I remember one particular therapy session when I was 24. My therapist, like always, started the session with "How are you feeling?" I began to explain "I think there is something wrong with me. I feel funny." As she probed deeper I explained that I had an overwhelming feeling that I didn't know how to respond to and I didn't know what it was. I was overcome with wiggly, tingly energy and I wanted to whistle a lot. She started to laugh and said "That is pure happiness." Without any external reference points I had been confused because I couldn't understand how that in 24 years of my life this was the first time that I was starting to feel happiness.

We usually learn to feel and express happiness at a young age. However, during my early years true happiness was not a safe emotion so I began asking everyone in my life how they expressed happiness. I eventually learned, as an adult, how to express happiness with a lot of help from my friends.

What are the benefits to being happy?

When we are happy the biochemicals, neurotransmitters and hormones that are released in our bodies promote general health and wellbeing. The side effects of happiness include longer life, better relationships, improved physical health, more energy, more pleasure and more positive experiences in your daily life. Some people even believe that happiness attracts financial abundance.

Take a moment and write down your happiness goals and how the different areas of your life can benefit. Once you are done I want you to turn your writings into a collage or poster. Take some time to be creative and have fun with it; colour and arts and crafts have a healing quality. Title your artwork "Happiness is my New Best Friend" and hang it on the wall where you can see it every day.

This exercise will help to create a daily reminder to keep you inspired and moving forward on the happiness train.

 All aboard!!! Choo Choo!

Another important benefit of Stop! Drop! & Wiggle! is that you will gain the ability to respond to life's events versus reacting to them. Let me explain this a little further. Being reactive means you are allowing life to happen to you; you react to life's events without thought, without cause and without choice. You are essentially in a prolonged triggered state. You feel powerless as if you don't have any choice in your life. When you start to practice Stop! Drop! & Wiggle! you will be armed with the knowledge that you are powerful and you will have the ability to take action and respond to life's events. You will gain awareness of when you are slipping into reactive patterns and you will be able to choose to respond differently. It's very empowering to feel in control of your life.

It's Time to be Silly

This is one of my favourite chapters because it's all about being silly! In order for Stop! Drop! & Wiggle! to be successful we need to look at your feelings, ideas and even your fears about being silly.

 Don't worry. Take a deep breath and take my hand. We're going to explore being silly together.

Have you ever noticed that as grown-ups we tend to only play, giggle and get downright silly when we're around small children or we've been drinking? When did our ability to be silly stop?

Have you ever felt that as grown-ups our ability to play, giggle and get downright silly begins to diminish? Perhaps our playfulness only comes out when we've been drinking, our guard is down and we lose our inhibitions? When did we lose our ability to be playful and silly?

For each one of us it stops at a different age or for a different reason but the one thing we all have in common is at some point in our lives we've all been told to "GROW UP!"

I'd like you to try an exercise. On one side of a piece of paper I want you to write the word grown-up and on the other side I want you to write the word inner child then I would like you to answer the following questions and put your answers under the appropriate heading…

Grown-Up Questions

What does it mean to be a grown-up?

What do grown-ups do every day?

What does a grown-up look like?

How does a grown-up behave?

What can a grown-up do for fun?

Are you a grown-up?

Do grown-ups laugh? And if so, when, where, and how long do they laugh?

Is being a grown-up a full time thing? Or Part time?

Do grown-ups act silly? And if so, when, where, and how often do they act silly?

When did you become a grown-up?

Inner Child Questions

Do you have an inner child?

What does your inner child look like?

When was the last time you played?

Do you let yourself explore the world through the eyes of a child?

What are you passionate about? Are you a very passionate person?

How often do express passion?

Do you Express creativity, passion or joy daily, weekly, monthly, or yearly ?

How often do allow yourself to create?

Our inner child is extremely important to our wellbeing. It is the voice inside all of us that is the source of wonderment, creativity, excitement, emotional centre, passion and blissful joy. When you suppress the inner child you cut yourself off from these important feelings which can be very emotionally, physically and psychologically unhealthy.

This exercise should give you some insight into how you visualize yourself and your inner child on a subconscious level. Do you embrace and welcome your inner child as part of your life or does the grown-up part of you see your inner child as something to be suppressed?

 There are no wrong answers. You are just the non-judgemental observer.

If you look unfavourably on your inner child you are not alone. Most of us have been raised with the idea that we are all supposed to work hard to become serious, mature grown-ups; that is the end goal. When we accomplish this goal we will be considered successful and we will gain the approval of our parents and our social peers. We will finally be allowed to eat at the "adults' table". The problem with this idea is that we often believe that in order to accomplish this we have to deny or squash our inner child. This leaves us feeling empty and numb inside.

That is why so many people are faced with a mid life crisis and can do some pretty extreme things just to feel alive again.

Did you know that you can still be a grown-up while embracing your inner child? I like to describe it as being a playful adult.

Here's how I decided to became a playful adult...

It was the night of my 18th birthday. I was completely freaking out and in a panic I turned to my best friend and said "I cannot become a grown-up. If I do I think I will die!"

To me becoming a grown-up meant all the fun, play, laughter and adventure would cease to exist as part of my daily life. It was a core belief that you were only allowed to be silly and playful when you were drinking or you were around children. I did not see many opportunities as a "grown-up" for silliness because I was not much of a drinker and I knew that having children was not in my future.

It was in that moment that I had a revelation. I made a conscious decision that I was not going to become a "grown-up". To me a "grown-up" was simply a social condition to suppress one's inner child. I was going to become a PLAYFUL ADULT. I would know when it was important to be responsible and serious but I could be free to spend the rest of my time being light, playful and silly.

I can happily say that I have embraced my inner child without compromising my adult responsibilities and for the last 20 years I have been teaching others to do the same.

 So! Do you want to continue to be a serious, miserable grown-up or will you choose to become a playful adult?

Alright then! Now you are ready to become the playful adult that you were meant to be. Here is an exercise to get you started:

 WoooooHoooo!!!!

Playful Adult Exercise

- Go to the bathroom then close and lock the door so you are alone.

- Next, look in the mirror and make the craziest silly face you can think of.

- Allow yourself to laugh and giggle without judgment.

- For the next week every time you are in front of a mirror I want you to make a different silly face.

- During those moments, allow yourself to giggle and feel the freedom of silliness flow through you.

- After one week, reflect back. Do you laugh more often in your life now?

Congrats! You have just allowed your inner child to play. Keep it up, because I promise you, it will lead to being a better adult, a better parent, a better friend, a better partner. It can even make your work more enjoyable.

You have taken your first steps to becoming the best darn Playful Adult you can be!

Alright, I think you are ready to start exploring the 7 steps of Stop! Drop! & Wiggle!

Here we go!

Let's Begin

We've talked about the history of Stop! Drop! & Wiggle! We've talked about the influences that allow us to be miserable. We've talked about what you have to look forward to. We've talked about how important it is to recognize and embrace your inner child. You have been very patient. So, congratulations! You've made it this far without giving up! And now you are ready to explore the 7 Easy Steps to Happiness.

 Way to go! You Are Awesome!!

In the following chapters we are going to explore each of the 7 steps of Stop! Drop! & Wiggle! In each chapter I will give you some insight into the history and purpose of each step and there are some exercises to help you along the way. With all this information I am about to share Stop! Drop! & Wiggle! may seem like a complicated process so in this chapter I am going to give you a very brief overview of the Stop! Drop! & Wiggle! program so that you can see the whole picture and can see how quick and easy it will be. After I have explained all 7 steps I will provide another summary with greater detail so you can reflect back on everything you have learned.

 Here we go!

Stop! Drop! & Wiggle! 7 Easy Steps to Happiness:

1. **STOP!** For 30 seconds fully express and explore your feelings.

2. **OBSERVE!** Just make a note of the stories that go along with your feelings.

3. **DROP!** This is the critical moment. Are you going to choose misery or happiness?

4. **WIGGLE!** Shake it 'til you giggle, then laugh for 60 seconds.

5. **GRATITUDE!** Two minutes dedicated to the things you are grateful for.

6. **LOVE!** List all the people, places and things you love.

7. **SHIT or Get off the Pot!** Let go and see the possibilities.

With these 7 easy steps you will be able to feel and acknowledge your unpleasant emotions without letting them consume you and then shift into true feelings of happiness. After that you will be able to let go of the things that are holding you back and see all the new possibilities. Dedicating about 5 to 10 minutes to Stop! Drop! & Wiggle! should be plenty of time to complete all 7 steps; so you have no excuse. The key is to practice the 7 steps every time you feel the unpleasant emotions taking control. This is how you will reprogram your default emotional expression from one of misery to one of happiness.

Remember it took many years to create your default emotional expression so in order to make lasting change you will need to be vigilant. And always remember to be patient and kind with yourself.

 Practice! Practice!! Practice!!! You can do it!

Step 1: STOP!

and let it all out

 For 30 seconds fully express and explore your feelings.

In this first step I want you to STOP! and do something different. If you've been caught up in an unpleasant emotion, you've been crying for an hour, you've been stomping around the house, you've been afraid to try something new I want you to STOP! If you've become overwhelmed by a sudden intense emotion and you're feeling uncomfortable or you find yourself lashing out I want you to STOP! If you've been avoiding your feelings, if you've been moping on the couch, if you've been avoiding going home from work I want you to STOP!

As soon as you make the choice to STOP! I want you to dig deep and become consciously aware of what you are feeling. As soon as you connect with those feelings I want you to set a timer for 30 seconds. You can use your watch, a stop watch, your phone, whatever is convenient. This might feel different from how you were expressing emotions before. Previously you were reacting but now you are consciously responding which over the long run will make it easier to let go of your unpleasant emotions.

It's important to follow the 30 second rule because many of us hold back unpleasant emotions or latch on to them unable to let go. In fact, the idea of truly feeling and acknowledging our emotions for 30 seconds can be a scary or difficult task for many of us. I believe our ability to express emotions falls into two categories.

The Avoider: The avoider does not give themselves permission to feel their emotions and may be deeply afraid of feeling their emotions for a full 30 seconds. The fear can be so strong they can spend most of their life trying to avoid feelings all together.

The Processor: The processor cannot accept that 30 seconds is long enough to truly process and feel their emotions. These clients often wear their suffering and misery like a badge of honour. Just like a warrior might see their battle wounds as part of their identity.

The Avoider

For the avoider there are a number of different reasons they react the way they do. As a child they may have been taught or shown that expressing their feelings was wrong or unsafe. For example, a little boy crying might have been repeatedly told, "Boys don't cry." Or another common message children have heard is "Stop crying or I will give you something to cry about." with the implied threat of physical harm. For some, showing their emotions creates a feeling of weakness and vulnerability. Others may fear that once the feelings start they may never be able to stop the intense emotions. For some avoiders there may have been someone in their life they do not want to emulate; perhaps it was someone who was physically or emotionally abusive when they expressed their emotions or someone who was an emotional victim and was always falling apart. Avoiders can also develop all sorts of ingenious coping strategies to avoid feeling and expressing their emotions all together. One of the most common coping strategies is addiction:

Here are some addictions you may be familiar with:

- Work
- Food
- Drugs
- Alcohol
- Relationships
- Love
- Sex

The next time you reach for your favourite addictions take a moment to ask yourself what are you trying not to feel?

The truth is, the more that you try to avoid your unpleasant emotion the harder your emotions fight to be released. When you avoid expressing your feelings in a safe and healthy way you simply create more crap, drama, crises and issues that are holding you down. Most avoidance coping strategies don't work in our best interest or in the best interest of the people around us-it's just a lot of smoke and mirrors. The emotions will always find a way, usually unhealthy, to be expressed. This even includes making our bodies sick. To become happy and content in your life you will eventually have to fix, change and experience these things. And the truth of the matter is that in the end you will still have to confront your emotions. Emotions always win! It's so much easier and less time consuming to take the 30 seconds to feel your emotions.

Now, repeat after me! "My emotions are NOT wrong! It is SAFE to feel them!"

Way to go! You rock!!

The Processor

The processor is someone who holds on to their unpleasant emotions never letting go of a negative experience. Processors often feel like 30 seconds is not enough time to fully experience their emotions. There are many reasons for this, for example:

Processors are often addicted to the reactions received from other people while they are expressing emotional distress: attention, pity, sympathy and even admiration for facing adversity. Some use this as a substitute for love, bonding and connection.

- Some processors are recovering Avoiders with years of back logged emotions. Now that the flood gates are open they do not know how to regulate them.
- Processors can be addicted to the biochemical rush that is released when experiencing intense unpleasant emotions.

- Being miserable can become a Processor's personal identity (think of Oscar the Grouch).

For some of us we use a combination of strategies; a processor in some situations and an avoider in others. For example you may hold on to an angry emotion for a long time but have difficulty expressing sadness. So please don't label yourself, look at each emotional expression independently.

Healthy Expressions

In some situations you will be able to fully express your 30 seconds of emotions in the moment (we'll talk more about building Stop! Drop! & Wiggle! friendly zones later in the book). In other instances it might not be possible, appropriate or safe to really get your emotions out. It's very important that you are able to express your emotions in a safe, healthy and effectual way. Many of us have not had good emotional role models so let's start from scratch.

Remember this simple rule: Bring no harm unto yourself or others. This means no yelling, screaming hitting, kicking, punching or biting directed at another person, child or animal; this is not healthy. No damaging other people's property or hurting yourself in anyway (verbally or physically) this also is not healthy.

Here are some ideas and tools for healthy release of some of your deep-seated or more intense emotions:

Anger

Anger requires a physical expression to be fully released otherwise you are suppressing it and it can turn inward into self hatred or ooze out into all other areas of your life even leading to abuse. Be sure to find a safe place to express your anger. This could be in your car or alone in your house. You can even take a trip out to a nearby forest or park. Now, you don't necessarily have to be alone, you may have someone supporting you in this process, but if you are doing this in the presence of others be sure that they will not feel intimidated or scared.

Some healthy methods you can use with Stop! Drop! & Wiggle! for releasing anger include, screaming or yelling at the top of you lungs, jumping up and down, hitting pillows, throwing rocks in a lake or river or throwing eggs into a bathtub or out in the forest.

Sadness

Tears are a healthy expression of sadness. If you feel them coming on do not try to stop them; crying is a beneficial process that rids the body of unwanted toxins. If you are worried about someone judging you simply find a private place and let the tears flow.

Fear

Fear is an emotion that triggers the fight or flight response in our bodies. Our fear response is one of our basic survival instincts. It was created to keep us alive and that is why our body, brain and nervous system go into the fight or flight response. However, on a daily basis, most of us are not in immediate life threatening danger. Over time our fear response has become psychologically linked to things like fear of failure, fear of success, fear of abandonment, fear of love and fear of powerlessness. Fear can also develop into phobias. If you are in true physical danger remove yourself from the situation. However, in most fearful moments you can simply look at the causes of your fear. What do you think could happen? Why does that frighten you? What do you think will happen? Who or what is causing you to feel this fear?

Here is an exercise to help you become more aware of your daily emotions. It will help you track your progress with Stop! Drop! & Wiggle!

Emotional Awareness Exercise

* Start a journal

- At the end of each day look at your emotions chart. (Emotions Chart, Appendix B.)

- See how many emotions you remember having throughout your day then write them down in your journal.

- Repeat for a couple of months.

- After a couple of months look back at your journal to identify any emotional patterns or changes.

There is a large spectrum of emotions for you explore and experience. The Emotions Chart, Appendix B, can be photocopied and posted on your wall for easy reference.

Emotional Check In

We are all familiar with the big emotions but sometimes our emotions are quiet and linger in the background like our default emotional expression. There may not always be a trigger alerting you that this is a good time to do the Stop! Drop! & Wiggle! steps. An Emotional Check In is a great tool to identify those moments when you are trapped in an unhappy emotion and may not be aware of it.

 Warning! Warning! Feeling Crappy!

To do an emotional check in set an alarm on your phone or watch. When it goes off do a quick assessment of your emotional state and your body language. You will learn to trust your body because it never lies to you when you know what to look for.

Emotional Check In Exercise

- Start with your emotional state and ask yourself, "How am I feeling in this moment?" You want to be in a positive emotional state. "Ok" or "fine" doesn't really count; they are neutral non-committed responses.

- Next do a body scan start with your toes and work your way up to your head and out through your fingertips. Look for any signs of unusual discomfort or muscle tension. Check your heart rate. Is it calm and steady, racing or irregular? How about your breathing? Is it slow and deep or are you holding your breath or breathing fast?

- You want to be in a relaxed state, happy and calm. I like to use the term Zen when everything is feeling right in the world. If you are feeling anything other than Zen this would be a good time connect with the emotions you are feeling. Once you do you can start Stop! Drop! & Wiggle!

Another great time for an emotional check in is when you find yourself reaching to a coping strategy or addiction. For example, if you are standing in front of that fridge or avoiding going home from work, dig deep, find the emotion and then take 30 seconds and explore what you are feeling.

Emotions are very powerful. They can seem like they have a mind of their own, which at times can be true but no matter if our emotions make sense or are irrational we must express them in healthy ways for short amounts of time. Remember that this step is no more than 30 seconds otherwise you are just indulging and reinforcing the negative emotional default that your life is awful and it sucks. When you give that much power to your unpleasant emotions you will continue to stay miserable and you deprive yourself of the happy life you desire to have.

Repeat after me:

My negative emotional default is not who I am. It is safe to be happy.

Now it is time to move to the next step. Don't get stuck in the emotions. I give you permission to let it go!!! You are amazing and I know you have it in you!!!

Step 2: OBSERVE!
what's your story?

Just make a note of the stories that go
along with your feelings.

Our emotional expressions are made up of two parts; the physical and the psychological. The physical is how our body reacts when we are feeling emotions. This can include muscle tension, tears, increased blood pressure, changes in our breathing patterns, sweaty palms, the shakes, increased heart rate, to name a few. These are normal and to be expected and can occur no matter what type of emotion you are feeling. It's part of your healthy emotional expression. These physical symptoms only become an issue when our default emotional expression is one of misery and our body is constantly under duress.

The psychological part lay in the stories we tell ourselves. This is where the brain shows up for the emotional party. While you are expressing your emotions in Step 1 there will be a number of stories going through your mind. They may be subtle or they may be big and loud and they will probably be in the form of a narrative about the situation or event. In the past you might not have even been aware of your stories. To help you understand what I mean by stories I would like to share a recent experience with you.

My life is generally very busy and I'd been having a crazy week. On top of it all I had just got a new puppy. Finding some time to sit down and work on this chapter was a bit of a challenge. I finally found a block of time and I was making some great progress right up until my computer crashed. I just lost everything. As you can imagine I was frustrated and angry. Here are the stories I told myself:

- The universe is out to get me!

- Technology hates me!

- Technology is not reliable!

- Damn I was dumb! I know better!

- I should have saved my work more often.

These stories are influenced by a number of underlying themes. For example: There are the Inner Critic Stories. These are the stories that are tied to self-doubt and self-hatred. We tell ourselves these stories because they support the negative core beliefs we have about ourselves. There are the Irrational Stories. These are the stories we tell ourselves to validate our feelings and they are usually attached to coping strategies and core beliefs about the world around us. They often include emphatic expressions like "always" or "never". This is also where we might express stories of mild to extreme paranoia like "The world is out to get me." Lastly there are our Situational Stories. These are the stories we tell ourselves when our emotional response is based purely on facts.

When you start observing your stories on a more conscious level you might be inclined to start analyzing the crap out of them or piling on all the negative judgements about yourself. Don't do it! It is very important at this stage that we do not reengage our emotional connection to these stories. This is a very tricky skill, unless you happen to be Buddhist. So practice staying impartial and non-judgemental; we do not want to get stuck in our unpleasant emotions or negative self-judgement.

 If you are not sure what I mean when I talk about staying impartial and non-judgemental, simply imagine your stories as words on a piece of paper. In this perspective there is no emotion or disapproval attached to the words. This is what you want to achieve.

The reason we observe our stories is to simply become aware of them so that later, in Step 7, you will be able to look back at these stories from a new, healthy and happy perspective. At that point we will explore how to change your Inner Critic Stories to positive ones, how to shake off your Irrational Stories and how to effectively address your Situational Stories.

For now, to complete Step 2 you simply want to make a note of your stories so that you can come back to them later. If it helps you can write them down or make an audio recording. If you are finding yourself becoming emotionally reengaged here is a technique I like to use to help remain detached.

Story Bubbles Exercise

- Select one of your stories.

- Imagine placing the words inside a large soap bubble.

- Watch as the bubble floats away from you.

- Repeat until you have exhausted all the stories you have told yourself in Step 1.

You're doing great. Now get ready to Drop!

Step 3: DROP!

eeny, meeny, miny, moe

 This is the critical moment. Are you going to choose misery or happiness?

This is the most crucial step of Stop! Drop! & Wiggle! This step is all about taking the plunge; making the choice to let go of the attachment to your negative emotion or to stay stuck and wallow in it. It's time to show your emotions who is boss!

I know you might be thinking, "That is easier said than done" and in the past I might have been the first one to agree with you. Now I know that I have the power to choose to continue feeling miserable or to choose happiness. You have the same choice!

Be ready for your negative emotional default to come up with all sorts of wonderful excuses as to why you should not listen to me or why you are justified to stay miserable. It wants you to stay stuck. It wants to maintain the status quo because that is what is safe and familiar. Don't listen to it!

Only by making the choice to let go can you move to a new place of happiness where you can focus your positive energy on seeing new possibilities.

 It's so much easier to see and create new opportunities when you are in a place of happiness and not distress. Happiness creates hope. Hope creates possibilities. Possibilities create action. Action creates your happy life.

We're about to take the plunge! Take my hand and we'll jump off the cliff of suffering and dive into the ocean of happiness!

Wheeeeeeee!!!

Ok, maybe you're a little nervous. Feeling stuck? One way that helps me get unstuck is to admit to myself that I am willingly holding on to my misery. I know, after everything we've talked about it sounds crazy but just wait while I explain.

If I get stuck I simply say out loud, "I enjoy being miserable!!!" Sounds crazy right? Absolutely!! But as I say it out loud I am forcing my conscious self to confront my subconscious behaviours. My conscious self KNOWS this statement is NOT true. This is usually enough to strengthen my resolve and to make the choice to DROP! This is the moment for you to become the master of your happiness. No more waiting for other people to make you happy. No more expecting external events and experiences to make you happy. YOU are the master of your happiness in each moment of your day.

Repeat after me: I am the master of my happiness.

Again, louder! I am the master of my happiness! Excellent!

Louder!! I AM THE MASTER OF MY HAPPINESS!!!

Great! Now you are ready for step 4. Wiggle! until your face hurts.

Step 4: WIGGLE!
until your face hurts

I'd like to tell you how I discovered the power of the Bum Wiggle. It all started with my Aussie Sheppard named "Tie". When he was happy he would start to wiggle his bum but because he didn't have a tail his whole bottom would wiggle and it would make me giggle every time. One day I was cuddling with my awesome, sexy husband and in that moment I was so filled with joy and happiness that without thinking I started to wiggle my bum.

My puzzled husband asked, "What are you doing?" And I told him, "Expressing my happiness like Tie does with a bum wiggle". We both laughed so I said, "You should try it." and he did! Since then when either one of us is super happy we wiggle our bums. It has become one of the non-verbal ways we express our happiness in the world.

 My husband is a big, burly, construction worker. So if HE can do it and still keep his burly man image there is no excuse for you not to try!

Tie passed away in the summer of 2013.
I'd like to take this moment to thank Tie for teaching me the power of the Bum Wiggle. In honour of Tie's memory let's do a Bum Wiggle right now!

The next time the Bum Wiggle made a profound entrance into my life was at my pottery and drumming studio. I was teaching a children's class when I met an amazing seven year old girl with Autism that would change my life forever. It was my first experience teaching someone with special needs and I was looking for a way to engage this little girl.

At the end of our first class we had music and drumming time and I noticed that she was able to remember the hand motions that went along with the song. I wondered if I could use this method to teach her a pottery technique for joining two pieces of clay. So in our next class I tested a theory; I created a little song with dance moves and it went like this:

Scratch, scratch
Water, water
Squish and wiggle.

The technique was a hit! All of the kids wanted to participate. They seemed to love doing it and it helped them remember the steps. I started using this technique with all my students including the adults. What I discovered was that everyone would smile and giggle when they had to do the Bum Wiggle. Sure, they may have been shy at first but I fostered a safe and non-judgemental environment and so their apprehension didn't last long. I saw huge shifts in my students' emotional states especially my adult students. They would often come into the studio stressed and grumpy but once they started to bum wiggle their crappy moods vanished and they became happier.

I realized it is super hard to stay miserable and crabby when you are wiggling your bum!!

Alright! Give me another bum wiggle right now! Let yourself giggle . Shake your booty... shake it ... wiggle ..wiggle...

If you have a physical difficulty that prevents you from wiggling your bum, any silly movement will do. You can try wiggling your nose or ears. Jazz hands are a great alternative. It's all about silly movements that make you giggle and laugh.

Now I know some of you might not be ready yet. You might be feeling like there is no way you can just wiggle your bum, maybe it feels dumb or stupid. Maybe you are feeling one of the following fears:

- What if someone sees me, what will they think?
- That is just TOO silly.
- That is childish and I am a grown-up.
- It's not proper to be silly like that.

Here is my response to your fears:

- If someone sees you, be an inspiration of happiness.
- Yes it is silly and silliness is a part of expressing happiness.
- Yes, it is child like and your inner child wants to play, if you let it.
- Everyone has an inner child that needs time to play.

Worrying about being proper is hindering your ability to express happiness.

 I KNOW you want to be happy because you are reading this book. So shake off the shackles and wiggle your bum!

I want to share a great Bum Wiggle moment I had while writing this book.

I was at the bank one morning and using a typical greeting the teller asked, "How are you today?" I went on to tell her that I was "Fabulous!" She smiled politely and asked how it was that I could feel fabulous this early in the morning. (Recognize the socially acceptable default to choose misery?)

I told her it was the Bum Wiggle! She looked at me rather puzzled and asked, "What do you mean, Bum Wiggle?" So in front of the WHOLE bank I showed her! She started to giggle and said, "That looks like fun."

So I conspiratorially whispered, "You can try it too." And she DID! She gave me a great big booty shake! We both giggled and laughed and afterwards she thanked me for the Bum Wiggle.

> The most profound moment of this experience was when I turned around to see all the smiling faces where there had been blank, glazed over looks previously. A little bit of happiness goes a long way!

We can make the world around us a better and happier place when we risk being happy and silly. My own experience has been that my expressions of happiness and silliness almost always inspire others to smile or join in. So, don't be afraid to express your happiness with your body or words. It's more likely that your happiness will be infectious and less likely that it will result in you being judged.

The only time I've really felt judged is when I wasn't secure in my own feelings. I realize now that I was subconsciously looking for someone to validate my hesitation so I could say "See, it is not safe for me to express my happiness." Bullshit! If you look hard enough you will always find someone to reinforce your insecurity.

When other people judge you it really has nothing to do with you. People judge others because:

- they fear not being good enough themselves.
- they are angry that you have chosen happiness. To accept that you are right means they are wrong and this is scary.
- they were told "You cannot behave that way." So if they can't why can you?

When you realize that other peoples' judgements are not a true reflection of who you are but rather who THEY are then the fear of judgement should no longer be able to hold power over you.

Remember if you are still fighting your fear of judgement just picture my burly husband or some other unlikely person wiggling their bum like crazy and let the mental image inspire you to take the risk and then WIGGLE! Practice your bum wiggle right now! Wiggle! Wiggle! Wiggle!

I hope this new knowledge has given you the permission and the freedom to wiggle your bum at home, at school, at work and even while standing in line at the bank.

But Gaia, why do you want us to bum wiggle?

 It's to help you laugh of course!

For most people we only feel safe laughing if something external happens to trigger that laughter, even then we are often conditioned to only express "socially appropriate" laughter. Unbridled knee-slapping, belly-holding laughter is only permitted under the right circumstances. Some people have even learned to suppress their laughter because they were teased or bullied at some point in their lives.

Three years before Stop! Drop! & Wiggle! was created I was in the jungle of Costa Rica playing a game called "Abounding River, The Game of Being Abundant" with a group of local women.

In the game when a player lands on a certain square all the players had to laugh for 60 seconds. The first time someone landed on the square I became very self conscious. Before this moment, I had never thought about or even cared about how my laughter would sound. By the second time someone landed on the square I started to notice a change in my body. My body started to tingle and the longer I laughed the happier I became. I let go of all of the worry and simply embraced the laughter. I felt as light as an air bubble. This was very important moment in my life. This is when I learned that laugher was a powerful ingredient in creating happiness.

When we laugh it changes our brain chemistry and our bodies start to produce all sorts of feel good hormones as well as reducing many of the negative hormones associated with stress. This is why it is very important to laugh for at least 60 seconds to really allow these changes to become present in our bodies. Plus it is very hard to stay miserable when you are laughing.

> Did you know that by holding in all that laughter you have been denying yourself joy, feel good biochemicals and good bowel movements? That's right, the more you laugh the happier your bowel movements will be.

> Many years ago a very popular Canadian healthy living television campaign called "Body Breaks" did a segment on laughter and bowel moments. As a kid I thought this was just about the funniest thing I'd every heard; they were talking about laughing and pooping on TV.

> Come on! I'll bet that made you laugh too!!

OK! It's time to practice. I know it seems hard and you might feel a bit silly and self conscious but it's OK. No one will judge you. Go ahead, let's try it together.

Give me a little bum wiggle to warm up. Are you feeling it yet? No? Ok, keep wiggling. Come on I know you can do it! Now, find your inner child and give me a "HA-HA-HA!"

Go for it! Laugh from the bottom of your belly. Let out your inner cackle. Try as many different types of laughter as you can and then just let it take over.

If you are struggling with laughing, here is an exercise:

Free Your Laugh Exercise

- Find some place no one can hear you (for example: in your car, in the forest, in your house).

- Now think about some past moment in your life that made you laugh.

- Let the laughter build.

- Think of someone that made you laugh.

- Let the laughter build.

- Think of a funny movie moment.

- Open your mouth and let the laughter out HAHAHAHAHA!

This step is really important because it allows you to complete the process of letting go of your unpleasant emotions so that you can begin the next stage of healing and keeping your emotional default healthy and happy.

Step 5: GRATITUDE!
is the best attitude

Two minutes dedicated to the things you are grateful for.

When we take for granted all the amazing little things that make up our lives it's no wonder we feel miserable. It's easy to believe that life sucks and that things are hopeless. Taking two minutes to express gratitude can help change these default subconscious emotions.

It's almost impossible to still feel helpless, miserable and like your world just sucks after two whole minutes of gratitude. Gratitude is a very powerful tool.

- It helps put our lives in perspective.
- It allows us to see how truly wonderful life is.
- It is the antithesis to our negative emotional default of misery and self pity.

 I have found that the more grateful you are, the more wondrous and amazing things can come into your life.

Now if you think there is no way you could fill up two whole minutes with things you are grateful for I'm here to tell you that is a whole bunch of hooey. Gratitude is not just about the big things like a great job, lots of money, an awesome marriage, a loving family, a big house, fabulous cars and so on. It's also about all the little things like:

- I woke up today.
- I have feet.

- I can see, taste and smell.
- I have clothes to wear.
- I have a roof over my head.
- I have food in my fridge.
- I have a fridge.
- Etc.

You get the point! As long as you are alive you have plenty of stuff to be grateful for and it's time to stop taking your life for granted. In North America our very consumer oriented culture teaches us to feel like we don't have enough and our lives are incomplete; this is the power of consumer advertising. So that is why it is important to express gratitude and remind ourselves that life is truly wonderful.

If you take a broad look at the world you can always find someone who is not as fortunate as you.

This is a fantastic moment to take a minute to be grateful for life. It might have been a while since you have allowed yourself to be thankful. So take a deep breath, close your eyes and think about 4 things in this moment that you are grateful for. Nicely done!

Expanding Your Gratitude Awareness Exercise

- Choose one thing you are grateful for.

- Expand on that item. For example, if you are grateful for an apple you are about to eat trace it back to its source of creation. Be grateful for the grocery store, the apple farmer, the truck driver, the rain and so on.

You get the idea!

In this step it is important to stretch your mind, to really embrace all the things that you have to be grateful for which you have kept buried deep in your subconscious (where you have been ignoring them). Use this opportunity to push out the unpleasant feelings and replace them with positive feelings of gratitude.

So now, by the end of step 6 you should be feeling pretty happy and excited about your awesome life. Don't fret if you are not quite there yet. It just means that you are super attached to those unpleasant emotions. Let's take a look at the next step.

Step 6: LOVE!
will set you free

 List all the people, places and things you love.

I like to call this last step the Big Kahuna because I believe there is no negative emotion so strong that it cannot be abated or completely evaporated by love.

Before we continue I'd like to answer the question "What is love?" I am not talking about romantic love or Hollywood love. I am talking about deep unconditional love.

What is unconditional love? Unconditional love is known as affection without any limitations. It is a love where you do not want anything in return. You have no desire to change the thing, person or place; it is perfect as it is. If you are still unsure what I mean think of the love you have for a child or a pet. That is unconditional love.

Some people are afraid of love. For a lot of us "love" can be a very scary word or concept because of unhealthy childhood experiences devoid of unconditional love. Then as we grow and become teenagers and young adults we experience romantic love relationships which can be very deep, powerful and usually heartbreaking with little or no unconditional love in them.

Our hearts get broken again and again and to protect ourselves we either close off completely from love or just allow a small trickle of love into our lives. Others can become addicted to love and engage in numerous short relationships that only last through the "honeymoon" phase.

The honeymoon phase is the stage in a relationship when all the excitement, adrenalin and endorphins of a new relationship are pumping through your body and your brain. This is when the fantasy that your ideal Hollywood love/soul mate is still a possibility. This honeymoon phase can also apply to business relationships and new friendships. It typically lasts from the first 3 weeks up to 6 months in a new relationship.

For people addicted to the honeymoon phase it is all about getting the next fix of adrenalin and endorphins or seeking the perfect but unachievable mate. It's a powerful addiction when you rely on these intense levels to exist in a relationship.

True unconditional love starts once the honeymoon phase is done and you can see the person as they really are including the good, the bad and the ugly and you still love them and want them in your life.

If you typically end or sabotage your relationships towards the end of the honeymoon phase then this is a sign you might be afraid of being in an unconditional love relationship. Alternately, love might be a scary thing for you, you may not feel worthy of being loved unconditionally or perhaps you have never experience unconditional love. If any of this rings true for you, I would recommend reaching out for some professional support, therapy or coaching to heal these old wounds.

We've talked a lot about coping strategies and core belief systems. Most of our negative emotional defaults started from a lack of unconditional love. If we feel like we are unworthy of experiencing and expressing unconditional love then how are we worthy of experiencing or expressing happiness.

 I know...DEEP!

Each time you practice step 6 you are changing and healing your feelings about being worthy of love and in turn giving yourself permission to be happy.

You might feel like you don't have many people, places or things that you love in this world. That is OK. Just remember that your love list does not have to be made up of big things; the small stuff is just as important and each time you practice Stop! Drop! & Wiggle! maybe you will be able to add something new to the list.

This is an example from my love list:

- I love my husband.
- I love monkeys.
- I love berries.
- I love dancing.
- I love snicker-doodles.
- I love the Amazon rainforest.
- I love the sun.

Keep going until you are filled with all the things you love. It might take only 3 things or it might take everything you can think of for your emotions to shift. It all depends on how deeply you are attached to the unpleasant emotion. Feel free to repeat things on your list, just remember to keep going until you feel happiness.

Here is a little project to help you build your love list.

My Love List Exercise

- Get a pen and paper.
- Make a list of all the people, places, things you love.
- Start each sentence with "I love _____."
- For example:
    o I love pizza.
    o I love rainbows.
- Post your love list somewhere you will see it every day.
- As you think of new items add them to your list.

If you are the creative type you can take this a step further and make a love collage using pictures of the people, places and things you love.

Taking a few moments to practice your love list can allow you to realize that your life is pretty awesome and filled with love. It can help heal your old love wounds on a deeper subconscious level.

Step 7: SHIT!
or get off the pot

 Let go and see the possibilities.

When we were kids, if my siblings and I started whining about how much our lives sucked my mother would say, "Shit or get off the pot. If you are not happy with things the way they are then make a new choice." Her message was that you have the power to do things differently and only you have the power to make your life better.

Well, you're almost there! You've experienced and felt your emotions in a healthy way, you've wiggled until you've laughed and you've done some deep healing and now that you are in a healthy, happy place you can look back at the situation causing you misery and find new and lasting solutions.

Remember back in Step 2 when I told you we were going to come back to your stories? Now is the time for you to take a new look at the situation and we use our stories to help us to identify how we can respond differently.

 Back in Step 2 if you put your stories into bubbles you can take this opportunity to pop your bubbles and take a new look at your stories.

It often helps to look at a problem or situation using a third party perspective. Pretend you are watching a scene in a movie without any personal attachment to the plot or characters or try imagining yourself putting on a pair of magic glasses that will help you see new possibilities and different outcomes. Another great technique is to pretend you are watching a live version of a "choose your own adventure book." Watch the event unfold and choose potential variations.

The goal of this step is to dispense with the things that are holding you down so that you can see all the different possibilities so that nothing that can stand in the way of your happiness.

Let's use a hypothetical scenario to explore this step further.

In this scenario a married couple, Ann and Bob, have an agreement that Bob is to take the trash to the curb each week but for the last month it has not been done and the garbage is starting to pile up. Ann is feeling anger and disappointment that Bob has not honoured the arrangement. Ann has practiced her Stop! Drop! & Wiggle! steps and here are the stories she told herself:

a) I can't trust anything that comes out of his mouth.
b) He doesn't love me anymore.
c) Why can't he see how important this is?
d) This is driving me nuts.
e) I'm just a freak for feeling this way.

Assume, for now, you are Ann in this scenario but because you have on your magic glasses you are looking at this from an outside perspective. We do this because we don't want to go back to the unpleasant emotions and it is easier to remain objective when looking at someone else's situation.

 How often do you find it easier to give other people advice versus looking at your own crap?

Remember that our stories can be broken up into three categories; Inner Critic, Irrational and Situational. Depending on the situation you may tell yourself only one or two types of stories or you may tell yourself all three.

Using the above scenario let's attempt to identify each type of story and what you can do with it.

We'll start with the Inner Critic Stories. Our Inner Critic spends a lot of time judging us and it reinforces and validates the negative feelings and impressions we have of ourselves. It can be very strong but it will not help you to find solutions to the things in your life that are causing you misery. It will interfere and sabotage your happiness and over-all well being. The Inner Critic feeds your negative emotional default and it is like being followed around by a mean, disrespectful and disapproving person that you cannot get away from.

Here are some examples of self judgement or negative self talk:

- I am stupid.
- I can never get things right.
- I'm not good enough.
- I'm not pretty enough.
- I'm not strong enough;
- and so on.

Your Inner Critic is all about self hatred and self doubt stories and these stories can play in the back of your brain like a song on an endless loop. Your Inner Critic is just mean! It was developed and fine tuned a long time ago by experiences and outside sources; people or things that made your feel like you weren't good enough.

A good way to recognize stories from your Inner Critic is to ask yourself "If I said that to someone else would it make them feel good and supported or bad and miserable?" Why would you want to say something to yourself that you wouldn't say to others?

Can you identify the Inner Critic Story in our scenario above? If you said (e) you are correct. That is a great example of an Inner Critic Story.

Quelling the Inner Critic is an ongoing practice and over time you can reprogram you Inner Critic to become your Inner Cheerleader. It is so much better to have a positive and supportive friend with you than to have that mean, nasty, nagging voice following you around all the time. So when you find you Inner Critic creeping into your stories here is a reprogramming exercise to strengthen your Inner Cheerleader.

Create the Inner Cheerleader of Awesomeness Exercise

- When your Inner Critic says something nasty, stand up for yourself, take a deep breath and say "That's not true!"

- Visualize throwing the negative words into a bonfire or volcano. Our subconscious minds are strongly influenced by the things we visualize.

- Then choose an alternative positive message that is contrary to the negative message. Then repeat your new message three times.

Your new message doesn't have to be opposite; it just needs to be contrary, positive and supportive. For example:

- I am stupid. → I have the ability to solve this problem.

- I am fat. → I am beautiful just the way I am.

- I am useless. → I am valuable.

Don't forget to repeat it three times; it takes three times before your subconscious starts to accept the new message. Three times is the charm!

This is also an exercise that you should be using in those everyday moments when you might not be feeling an intense emotion but your Inner Critic is tossing out those insults. If you find yourself in a moment where you Inner Critic is making one of those disparaging remarks, initiate your Inner Cheerleader right away.

Now let's take a closer look at Irrational Stories. I like to call these stories Bat Shit Crazy Stories. These are probably the most popular stories we tell ourselves. Generally speaking these stories are not supported by facts but they can be difficult to identify because they often have multiple layers and we work very hard to believe them.

One day I was explaining the concept of Bat Shit Crazy Stories to a friend. She became very uncomfortable because she had spent most of her life coping with people calling her crazy. Remember this is just a term to help you smile and let go of your irrational stories. If the term bat shit crazy makes you uncomfortable you can use any silly terminology you like, just remember don't be judgemental (i.e. don't call them stupid).

I'd like you to consider this scenario: You are in your car heading to work. The kids are safely off to school and you are finally enjoying that first sip of morning coffee that you have waited patiently for in the long drive-through line up. As you pull out of the parking lot, out of nowhere, a car cuts you off and you spill coffee on your shirt. How do you respond?

- Do you spend the rest of the trip to work ranting about other drivers?
- Do you roll down the window and starts swearing at the other driver?
- Do you speed up to confront the other driver?
- Do you spend your day retelling the story to anyone who will listen?

If you answered yes to any of the above I am here to tell you that the other driver did not wake up that morning with the sole purpose of ruining your day. However, your intense emotional reaction suggests that deep down you may be telling yourself otherwise.

We use the stories we tell ourselves to support all sorts of emotional responses ranging from anger and rage all the way to paranoia (the world is out to get me). So in this situation what stories might you tell yourself? Here are some possibilities:

- What a jerk!
- He shouldn't be on the road!
- It's all his fault!

Take a moment to put these stories to the "Is it Real? Is it True?" test. Ask yourself are these stories real? Are they true? If the answer is "probably not" then there is a good chance that these are your Bat Shit Crazy Stories. So why do we tell them?

There are lots of reasons we tell them but generally speaking they may be masking a feeling we don't want to face or they support and validate our emotional default expression, our core beliefs or our various coping strategies. When we are feeling safe, happy and healthy we stop using our Bat Shit Crazy Stories.

Our Bat Shit Crazy Stories are not just for our intense emotional outbursts they also support to our passive emotions. Earlier we talked about addiction as a coping strategy. Consider the person who has a food addiction as a coping strategy and they are standing in front of the fridge deciding on what to eat. What stories might they be telling themselves?

- I am hungry!
- I'll feel better if I eat.
- If I don't eat that pie it will go bad.

If you put each of these stories to the "Is it Real, Is it True?" test what answers do you come up with? Our stories can be very tricky. For example, "I am hungry" might be true but in this example we may also be using it to support and validate our choice to eat even if we aren't truly hungry. Another possibility is these stories are covering up another unwelcome feeling like boredom, loneliness or stress.

It's very important to be as honest as possible with yourself at this stage. Many of your stories will be irrational because they are tightly linked to a trigger, a core belief, a coping strategy or your emotional default. Your subconscious will try to convince you that your stories are real and true because they fit your emotional programming.

We also use our Bat Shit Crazy stories to support and defend our pet peeves or as I like to call them Obsessive Compulsive Hiccups (OCH). Most of the time you can recognize an OCH when you have an emotional connection to something but you cannot understand why it doesn't affect others in the same way. For example; toothpaste should never be squeezed in the middle or the toilet seat should always be down (or up).

Let's go back to our first scenario with Ann and Bob. Can you identify the Bat Shit Crazy stories in this list?

a) I can't trust anything that comes out of his mouth.
b) He doesn't love me anymore.
c) He's a jerk for not seeing how important this is?
d) This is driving me nuts.
e) I'm just a freak for feeling this way.

This of course is a little harder because we don't necessarily have the same triggers, core beliefs and coping strategies as Ann. However, assuming that Bob is relatively trustworthy and he truly loves her I think we can safely say that (a), (b) and (c) are Ann's Bat Shit Crazy stories. Did you spot the OCH in this scenario? That's right. Taking out the garbage on time seems to be significantly more important to Ann than it is to Bob to the point that it is causing Ann misery.

It's important to remember that YOU are not bat shit crazy but sometimes our stories are because of the intense emotions that are attached to them. Our stories are not who we are.

 Remember your stories may be bat shit crazy but you are not.

There is one other emotion that I want to talk about briefly and that is hopelessness. One of the most deviant emotions that keeps us from making change is the feeling of being trapped and helpless, which leads to hopelessness. Once hopelessness sinks in we give up trying to make or lives better because we feel like "What's the point?" When you learn to look at every situation as having lots of possibilities and choices then you have the power to change what is not working and make it possible to choose happiness. When we put hopelessness to the "Is it Real? Is it True?" test…that's right, it's bat shit crazy!

The key to our Irrational Stories is to just laugh them off. When you find yourself looking back at your Bat Shit Crazy Stories the best thing you can do is just laugh and let them go. Take ownership for them and accept that they are irrational but deny them the power to control your life and your emotions. If it is something that you are very strongly connected to like an OCH then find solutions for the trigger but don't hold other people accountable for your stuff (in the long run you will be happier for it).

When I first started practicing Stop! Drop! & Wiggle! I was amazed at the number of Bat Shit Crazy Stories I told myself about everyday aspects of life. So now, when these crazy thoughts and behaviours creep into my life I have a personal label from them; it's Bat Shit #5. Each time I think of the phrase it makes me laugh and as a result the crazy thoughts and behaviours no longer have power over me.

Important Tip! As you pay closer attention to your daily emotional responses you might start to observe that you have some seriously "bat shit crazy" thoughts, feelings and reactions. (PS: This is not my fault!) Don't be afraid, this is natural. This is a normal phase of becoming self-aware. These behaviours have been present for a long time, you were simply not aware of them.

Over time this will become easier. Don't feel like you need to psycho-analyze yourself, it's not necessary. The purpose of this phase is to simply identify your Inner Critic and Bat Shit Crazy Stories so you can move past them. I promise that each time you practice this step you will gain a little more awareness of your emotional reactions which leads to understanding the triggers, core beliefs and coping strategies that may be attached to those reactions and over time you will start to reduce the number of Inner Critic and Bat Shit Crazy stories you tell yourself.

Remember don't spend a lot of time analyzing yourself, this is just a snap shot so that you can gain awareness of your stories long enough to laugh them off.

With awareness comes insight.

With insight comes empowerment.

With empowerment comes action.

With action anything is possible.

Before we look at Situational Stories, if you have gone back into the unpleasant emotions or you Inner Critic starts pointing out all your faults while you are looking at your stories it may be a good idea to start over at Step 4. Remember we are supposed to remain happy, impartial and non judgemental through this phase!

Once you have moved past your Inner Critic and Bat Shit Crazy Stories if there are any stories left those are your Situational Stories. Our Situational Stories are factual and based on the immediate event or circumstance. There is no attachment to past events or triggers, coping strategies or core beliefs. You might be surprised to learn that Situational Stories are only a small fraction of the stories we tell ourselves. In fact, don't be alarmed if there are no Situational Stories at all. It is quite common to have reactions that are based purely on our old coping strategies and core belief systems. If you have laughed off your Bat Shit Crazy Stories and spanked your Inner Critic then give yourself a pat on the back and go have some fun and enjoy being happy.

If there is a Situational Story left over you are now in a healthy, happy place in which to re-evaluate the situation that is causing you misery and discover new possibilities.

Let's look back one final time at Ann's stories. Can you spot the Situational Story?

a) I can't trust anything that comes out of his mouth.
b) He doesn't love me anymore.

> c) He's a jerk for not seeing how important this is?
> d) This is driving me nuts.
> e) I'm just a freak for feeling this way.

By process of elimination if you chose (d) you are correct. We can see that Ann has an OCH that is driving her nuts and the current solution isn't working so it's time to see that she has other possibilities.

Let's see if you can stretch your creative problem solving muscle. Grab a pen and paper and write down as many new possibilities for Ann as you can.

Done? OK, here are a few that I came up with:

- Talk to Bob (without anger or blame) and ask why he missed the trash last month. Maybe there is a simple explanation.
- Ann could hire a cleaner to take out the trash.
- Maybe someone else in the household would take responsibility for this chore.
- Maybe Ann would be happier if she did it herself.

How did you do?

Nice work!

Many of us have not been taught how to use creative problem solving skills so if you found this difficult here is a method you might find helpful.

Draw a circle in the centre of the page and inside the circle write down the problem you are trying to solve. Then draw a spoke outwards from the centre circle. At the end of that spoke write down a potential idea or solution no matter how crazy or unrealistic you think it might be and place a circle around the new idea. You can also use a new spoke to add any obstacles that come to mind. Use the same technique to find solutions for the obstacles. Effectively, you can draw a new spoke from any circle on the page so each circle can inspire new ideas. Once you see all the ideas on paper highlight the best option or the one you want to try next; when done it will look something like the example in Figure 1.

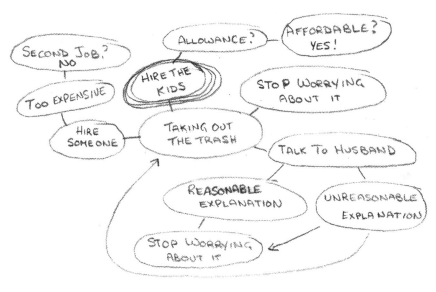

Figure 1

You can also turn this into an exercise or game that you can practice with your family.

Creative Problem Solving Exercise

Once a week create a hypothetical scenario and see how many different endings you can create with your new creative problem solving skills. When you are practicing use scenarios that you are not emotionally attached to so that it does not become emotionally charged and no one feels attacked.

The idea behind this exercise is to get you thinking outside your comfort zone and old patterns to create your new creative problem solving Super Power. Your new Super Power will show you that you are not stuck and things are not hopeless. You can find solutions for any situation in your life. Sometimes the solution can be simple acceptance and choosing happiness anyways.

 If you have an Inner Critic Story that keeps coming back or if you have a Bat Shit Crazy Story you just cannot seem to laugh off or an OCH is repeatedly causing you to lash out at people don't be afraid to consider seeking outside help as one of your potential solutions. You do not have to do this alone.

Let's do a recap of Step 7. Sort your stories. If you have any Inner Critic Stories awaken your Inner Cheerleader. Laugh off any Bat Shit Crazy Stories. Then, if you have any Situational Stories take a moment to consider some new possibilities.

Remember, you are the MASTER of your HAPPINESS!

Putting Stop! Drop! & Wiggle! into Practice

Create Stop! Drop! & Wiggle! Friendly Zones

It can be very helpful if you tell the people closest to you about Stop! Drop! & Wiggle! The more people who know the more safe places you will have to practice being a happier you. Having a safe place means the people around you understand that you are taking 10 minutes to do Stop! Drop! & Wiggle! and they are willing to give you the space to do it without interruption or judgement. It can also mean having an environment where you feel safe to practice Stop! Drop! & Wiggle! with other people in the room. It's all about where YOU feel safe.

Don't be afraid to tell people you are making a change for the better. Simply tell them you have found a great way to be happier in your life and you would like to share it with them then ask for their support. It will take some time to test the waters around you and share your newfound knowledge so that you can find and create your Stop! Drop! & Wiggle! friendly zones. Once you figure that out all you have to do is choose to use Stop! Drop! & Wiggle! whenever you are not feeling happy and relaxed.

You will find that most people will support you, but remember if you come across someone who is unsupportive or judgemental it has NOTHING to do with you. That person is just not ready to choose happiness. Simply smile and say, "I understand you might not be interested in this program but if you change your mind I would be happy share what I have learned." Then you can walk away or change the subject. They do not have power over you.

So if you find yourself in a non-friendly Stop! Drop! & Wiggle! zone simply excuse yourself and go to the bathroom or take a walk outside. You can go to your car or any other neutral place where you feel comfortable. Once you are feeling happy again then you can return.

Occasionally you might find yourself in a situation where you cannot excuse yourself for 5 or 10 minutes. In that situation take a deep breath and do a quick little bum wiggle to take the edge off. As soon as you have the chance do your emotional check in. If you are still holding on to the negative emotions do your Stop! Drop! & Wiggle! steps.

Share the Knowledge

One of the best ways to learn something is to teach it. Kids love Stop! Drop! & Wiggle! Teach your kids, teach your family. You can give your whole family a great tool for dealing with difficult emotions.

 The family that wiggles together stays together!

This past summer I was at the cottage with 4 of my 5 siblings. I love them dearly, but as you know sometimes sibling get-togethers can be stressful.

On the drive up I told my brother about this new program I was developing called Stop! Drop! & Wiggle!

On day two of our trip my brother and I were down at the dock enjoying a nice quiet fishing moment together when the rest of our sibling decided to come down and have a dance party on the dock. So much for quiet fishing!

When I looked over at my brother he was wiggling up a storm. I started to laugh like a crazy woman and started to wiggle myself! My brother and I were wiggling together and a sibling crisis was averted!

Thank you Stop! Drop! & Wiggle!

Practice Run

Now that you've read the book and you understand the how and why of each of the steps let's do a practice run through.

Let's start with your Emotional Check In. What's playing in the back of your mind? Are there any lingering feelings of unhappiness? Maybe you can focus on some specific unpleasant emotion or situation that has been troubling you.

Focus on identifying your emotions. Now you are ready for step 1…

Step 1: STOP! Find a safe place. Set a timer on your clock or your watch and for the next 30 seconds I want you to focus on those emotions. Go deep. Allow your emotions to fill you. Allow your body to physically react to the emotions.

Step 2: OBSERVE! As a non-judgemental observer make a note of your stories. Don't think about them or analyze them, just be aware of them. If it helps, you can record or write down your stories.

Step 3: DROP! Do you want to continue suffering or choose happiness? If you are not choosing happiness say to yourself "I CHOOSE to be _____." (Fill in the blank with your unpleasant emotion.) Sounds silly doesn't it? So what do you really want to choose? Happiness of course.

Step 4: WIGGLE! Start wiggling your bum. Come on I know you can do it. I see you smiling. Keep going until you start laughing. Now laugh for at least 60 seconds. You need that 60 seconds so do whatever it takes to keeps the laughter flowing. Fake it, make funny faces, think of funny movies or stories, whatever inspires you to laugh.

Step 5: GRATITUDE! For two minutes list out loud all the things you are grateful for-no matter how big or how small. Dig deep. If you are having difficulty, use your Gratitude Awareness Exercise.

Step 6: LOVE! Out loud, list all the people, places and things that you love until you feel joyful. This can be the smallest items or the largest. If you run out of things just repeat the list. The goal here is to fill your mind with the things you love.

Step 7: SHIT or get off the pot! Look back at your stories. Laugh at your Bat Shit Crazy ones and move on. If you have any Inner Critic Stories spend a moment to initiate your Inner Cheerleader. And then look to see if you have any Situational Stories and consider some new possibilities that will fulfill your new happy state. If the solutions are not obvious spend some time using your creative problem solving skills.

You have so much to look forward to once you start using Stop! Drop! & Wiggle! on a daily basis in your life. Here are just a few of the changes I've seen in myself:

People have started to notice that I am happier. Now when they ask me about it I can share my Stop! Drop! & Wiggle! experience and create a new Stop! Drop! & Wiggle! friendly zone.

I have stopped caring about what others think when I practice Stop! Drop! & Wiggle! If I need to laugh and wiggle my bum in public, I do. My happiness is more important that what others think about me. Most of the time people become genuinely interested in learning about the program.

I have become aware that my thoughts and emotional reactions to events are truly bat shit crazy a lot of the time. This has made it easier to shrug off those negative emotions attached to old belief systems.

You are Awesome!

I want to take a moment to celebrate just how truly awesome you are! That's right, I am talking to you! It takes courage, strength and will power to make a change. You are now on the path to making a lasting change in your life; to letting go of misery and embracing happiness.

 You Rock! Gimme a hands up! Woo! Woo!

But just in case you don't believe me-I know you are on the path to happiness because you've completed three important steps:

- You've picked up this book.
- You started reading.
- You finished reading.

Remember at the beginning of the book how you committed to reading the book all the way through? You did it! Awesome job!

Repeat after me:

- "I am AWESOME!"
- "I am COURAGEOUS!"
- "I say YES to HAPPINESS!"

Remember your second commitment, "I will practice Stop! Drop! & Wiggle! for two full weeks before deciding if this program is right for me."

It is time to take all this wonderful knowledge and put it into action starting today!

Remember every time you choose Stop! Drop! & Wiggle! you become even more amazing. You become a part of the elite group of individuals that are happy in the world. This makes you extra special and awesome!

This next exercise is my gift to you! I want you to remember each and every day just how truly awesome you are! What makes mantras and affirmations so powerful is that they help to reprogram negative emotional defaults and core belief systems.

Here is a great mantra exercise to help you to truly start believing you are amazing and awesome.

Mantra Exercise

- Go get some paper, coloured pencils, crayons or markers.

- Now create posters for each of the following mantras with big bold letters and your favourite colours.

  o I Am Awesome!

  o I Choose Happiness!

  o I Say Yes To Happiness!

  o I Am Incredible!

  o I Deserve To Be Happy!

  o I Am Worthy Of Happiness!

  o It Is Safe To Be A Playful Adult!

  o Laughter Is My Friend!

  o My Emotions Are Not Right Or Wrong. They Just Are!

  o It Is Safe To Feel My Emotions!

  o It Is Safe To Be Happy!

  o My Unpleasant Emotions Are Not Who I Am!

  o I Am Responsible For My Actions, Reactions And Choices In Each Moment!

  o I Am The Master Of My Happiness!

- If you don't have access to craft supplies you can do this on your computer as well. Just remember to print it in colour!

I want you to place these posters in prominent places in your life where you will see them everyday!

Each time you see your mantras I want you to read them out loud 3 times because every time you read them you are reinforcing just how fabulous you really are.

I believe it and so should you!

Tools for Life

In this chapter I want to provide you with some additional tools that will help you succeed on your journey to happiness. Some of them are directly related to Stop! Drop! & Wiggle! and some are great companion tools I have discovered along the way. I hope you find them helpful.

Grounding Meditation

This is a tool I was given years ago by my Tantra teachers Al Link and Pala Copeland from 4Freedoms. This is a very powerful companion tool that uses neuro-linguistic programming (NLP). Very briefly NLP is a therapeutic modality that uses the relationship between the mind (neuro) and language (linguistic) to affect our body and behaviours (programming). With this technique you will create an anchor point on your body, like your knee or your ring finger. After some practice when you touch this anchor point you will feel connected to the earth and you will be able to breath in the new calm, Zen and happy energy. You might think this sounds hokey but I'll tell you exactly what my teachers told me. Try this exercise every day for two weeks and then stop and see how you feel. See if you notice any difference in the way your life is going. I did and boy was I surprised and impressed with the results.

Grounding Meditation Exercise

- Turn off all electronics; your phone, your computer.

- Find a quiet space where you will be uninterrupted.

- Sit or lay down.

- Touch a spot on your body that will be your anchor point. Make sure this is a spot you will feel comfortable touching in public.

- Close your eyes. Do 10 Kegel squeezes (these are the pelvic floor muscles that you use to stop the flow of your urine).

- Start to visualize an image that connects your root chakra (this is your genital area) to the earth such as tree roots, a beam of light, a waterfall, a tube-it can be anything as long as it works for you.

- Imagine your image moving down towards the earth, through the floor, down through the first layer of soil all the way to the center of the earth where there is a large beautiful cavern filled with a pool of lava.

- Remember to breathe slowly, fully and deeply throughout the exercise.

- Once you have formed a connection from your root chakra to the centre of the earth let go of all you pain, sadness, worry, fear, shame, guilt, anger, tiredness, anxiety, stress and any thoughts, emotions or physical symptoms that no longer serve you.

- Allow them to flow through your connection down to the lava pool where you can watch them burn away. Remember to breathe.

- Once you have let everything go and watched it burn away take a deep breath in while doing a Kegel squeeze and allow warm, loving, calming, energizing and sexy energy move up from the centre of the earth into you.

- Keep breathing and squeezing to bring mother earth's energy into you until every cell is filled with it. Be sure to include your fingers, toes, nose, ears and right to the ends of your hair.

- Then open your eyes and continue with your day in a relaxed and joyful state of mind.

Do this at least once a day to bring calm, Zen and sensuality (or juiciness) into your life.

Remember to pick the same anchor spot on your body every time.

Saying Yes in the Morning

Starting your day off with a positive vibe can make a world of difference in how you spend the rest of your day. Many of us wake up to a loud obnoxious alarm clock that leaves us feeling miserable and already dreading the day. When you start off like that how is your day ever going to be awesome and filled with wonderment? Since I've changed my morning routine to include this exercise I've seen profound changes in the magnitude of positive events that I experience throughout my day.

Saying Yes in the Morning Exercise

- Change your alarm clock to one that uses pleasant, happy sounds. No more alarms that sound like we are under attack.

- When you wake up don't jump out of bed. Take some deep breaths and stretch.

- Then say to yourself 3 times "Today is going to be a _____ day!" Choose a word like awesome, fabulous, great, epic or wondrous.

- Now you can get out of bed and start your day off right with a great positive attitude.

If you are not a morning person and this doesn't quite get you over the hump write your morning statements on a piece of paper and post them next to your mirror in the bathroom. When you are in the bathroom for your morning routine look in the mirror and repeat your statement out loud.

Theta Meditation

I would like to introduce you to a tool that has helped change my life and it is called Theta Meditation. It was pivotal in eliminating my constant state of fight or flight response. For the first time in 37 years I was truly relaxed and calm.

Theta Meditation is a simple technique that involves listening to a specially formulated recording on CD or MP3 daily.

Pierre Black a wonderful Naturotherapist specializing in Chinese, Ayurvedic and Naturopathic medicines and my guide to health was kind enough to provide me with his insight into the emotional, physical and spiritual benefits of Theta Meditation (email to author, January 31, 2014).

States of stress primarily involve the beta range of brain frequencies. In these states, stress hormones such as cortisol and adrenaline are released. These hormones are harmful in excess. Digestion, assimilation, and elimination are impeded; tissue repair, immunity, glycemic and inflammatory modulation are all negatively impacted. What does this really mean? Most major degenerative diseases, so called "diseases of lifestyle", and diseases of aging are predicated on these factors: dysmodulation of immunity, inflammation, glycemia, and acid/alkali balance.

In not adequately managing stress, we train our brains toward chronic states of anxiety, hyper-vigilance, sadness, obsessive thinking, and other dysfunctions; over-training the brain and nervous system much in the same way we might over-train a muscle group. When we over-train toward chronic stress and discontent instead of training toward presence, self-knowledge and joy, we have created an imbalance which will eventually result in an experience of ill health, whether physical, mental, or spiritual.

Relaxation should be part of every day. True relaxation is a measurable brain state; the theta brain state allows the best assimilation of nutrients and body tissue repair, as well as the greatest reduction in the production of health-damaging stress hormones. Most modern city dwellers do not spend nearly enough time in the theta brain frequency range.

Meditation or Skilled Relaxation in various forms have been used throughout history for their positive effects on overall health and sense of well-being. Prayer, mantra, chanting, and meditation are only a few of many names used across time and culture, for techniques with essential similarities: an increase in parasympathetic physiology with movement toward theta range frequencies. These effects are often immediate and scientifically measurable. This confers far reaching effects on all aspects of physical, mental, and spiritual health. One experiences a more relaxed, healing, and creative state in which excessive analytical

thinking quiets, physiological stress patterns in the body calm, conflicts and traumas resolve, nutrients are better assimilated, and the body repairs itself more efficiently.

Low-Theta is the brain frequency achieved by experienced meditators and in conscious-dreaming during deeply relaxed states (not to be confused with lucid dreaming, which involves delta frequencies – true sleep). Spending more time in the low-theta brainstate promotes creative, personal and spiritual insights that cannot be achieved in other brainstates. Most modern urban people spend little or no time in this state.

I highly recommend incorporating Theta Meditation into your life. There are many suppliers out there but because this is your brain we're talking about I recommend a trusted producer like Brain Sync. You can obtain their CDs or MP3s through my website at www.succulentliving.com. They are relatively inexpensive and well worth the investment.

Emotional Tools

As fabulous as Stop! Drop! & Wiggle! is it might not work for every situation. If you have difficulty expressing your emotions or your emotions are scary for you these tools may help you learn to express and connect with your emotions in a healthy way. As you get better at navigating your emotions it will be easier to apply the Stop! Drop! & Wiggle! steps.

Anger Management

Shortly after I closed my pottery and drumming studio my sister Sarah Morrissette-who was also one of my instructors and Energy therapist-began to notice that since she had stopped working at the studio she was angry all the time. What we realized was that as a primal drumming and pottery studio we spent a lot of time in physical expression through drumming and the throwing and slapping of clay. We went on to discover that we really benefited by having an anger release visit once a week to help

let go of all those little events that might not be a big deal in the moment but they accumulate over time. This is the anger release exercise that we developed for just this type of thing.

Therapeutic Rock Throwing Exercise

- Find a secluded spot by a body of water.

- Visualize a large clear bubble around you about 50ft in diameter. This is your protection bubble and all of your anger will be contained inside this bubble where it cannot ooze out towards anyone you might be angry at.

- Pick up a rock and throw it.

- Pick up another rock. This time when you throw it grunt or make some other form of sound.

- Pick up your next rock. This time use words instead of sounds use words-swear words are fine.

- Before you throw your next rock allow yourself to vent, bitch or complain out loud. Say whatever is on your mind; do not filter or try to be polite then throw the rock.

- Repeat until you feel like you have exhausted that one issue you are angry about.

- Now say the following "By the power of the rock and the water so shall it be!" As you make this statement I want you to make a silly "Whoohoo" sound while doing a little hip shake.

- You can repeat this process for each thing that is causing you grief.

Once you have vented and released all your anger it is now time to pick up about 10 little rocks and allow each rock to represent what you are grateful for in your life. Say each one out loud and then throw the rock into the water. With each statement of gratitude say "By the power of the rock and the water so shall it be!" along with a "Woohoo" and a hip shake.

Learning to Cry

For some of us crying is hard to do. Here is a great tool to relearn how to cry so that you can clean out those tear ducts and physically release the sadness.

Start a journal and ask yourself "Why am I sad?"

If you come up with no answers think of something that made you cry in the past like a movie, commercial or card.

Once you get the tears flowing come back to the sadness in the moment and start Stop! Drop! & Wiggle!

Facing your Fears

When you body switches into fight or flight mode because of true fear it is important to pull yourself out as fast as you can. If you are in true physical danger then remove yourself from the danger immediately. If there is no physical danger you need to calm your nervous system. Extended exposure to the adrenaline and biochemicals of the fight or flight response can cause long term health problems. Here are some tools I have used for dealing with fear.

First step is to identify whether you are experiencing true fear or psychological fear.

As soon as your heart rate spikes and you start breathing rapidly or holding your breath, stop and ask yourself "Am I in immediate life threatening danger?" If the answer is yes remove yourself from the danger. If the answer is no take a deep breath and use a visual statement that eases your fears.

For example: If I get nervous about public speaking just before I go on stage I say out loud "The crowd is not going to stone me or chase me and try to eat me."

Your visual statement should be so ridiculous that you start to laugh. Because, as you remember, laughter changes the biochemical responses in your body and can help calm your nervous system.

Grounding Meditation and Theta Meditation are also great tools for dealing with fear.

Appendix A

In this appendix you will find several important concepts I have discussed throughout the book. I hope you will find the additional information interesting and helpful.

Core Belief System

Our core beliefs make up who we are. They define how we perceive and navigate the world around us. For example you can have a core belief that you are a lovable, likeable person and you will respond to other people accordingly; you may be easily approachable, friendly and outgoing, etc. Now if you have a core belief that you are not a loveable, likeable person you might respond to other people by avoiding contact, apologizing for yourself all the time, you might have low self esteem or body image issues.

We behave in ways which validate our core beliefs. For example someone who believes they are unworthy of love may choose friends who treat them poorly or choose a partner who is abusive because deep down they don't believe they deserve anything better.

We can have core beliefs in all areas of our lives. We can have core beliefs about ourselves, about other people, places, things, religion; anything that you believe deep down in your core regardless of whether or not you know why you believe it. But it is our negative core beliefs that hurt us. So if you can start to shift your old negative core beliefs into new positive ones you will begin to move through the world in a new way.

One of the benefits of Stop! Drop! & Wiggle! is its power to systematically change your core beliefs by reinforcing that you are worthy of love, that you can choose to be happy, that suffering does not need to be your emotional default and that it is safe to be happy in the world. Developing new healthy core beliefs will affect how you eat, how you sleep, what you do in your life, what jobs you choose and what type of relationships you will have and you will begin to validate your new, positive core beliefs.

Coping Strategies

If our core beliefs define how we see and navigate the world around us our coping strategies are how we deal with the world around us. It is the basis to how we respond to things that cause us stress. Many of our coping strategies are developed during childhood and they can be formed by observation-seeing how a parent responds to stress-or by natural discovery. During our childhood we learn how to respond to stress and unpleasant situations by developing methods to protect ourselves.

For example we may learn to withdraw from others to avoid being hurt. Acting out violently towards others may be a way to assert oneself. Self harm and suicidal tendencies can be a cry for help. These are all forms of coping strategies. Another form of coping strategy we discussed earlier was addictions. We can use various additions to hide and bury our painful and stressful emotions.

Consider this: A child who is embracing and enjoying life by dancing playfully on the playground is confronted by another child or adult who tells them "You're being stupid, stop that!" The stress and humiliation of the situation is overwhelming and the child develops a core belief that it is not safe to dance in public. Later in life when that same child is confronted with an opportunity to dance they are feeling the stress created by their core belief and they choose a coping strategy such as withdrawing or making fun of others as a way to cope. The funny thing about coping strategies is that because they were developed while we were children they have about as much sophistication as we did at that age.

One way I suggest for dealing with coping strategies is to imagine them as a child who is very sneaky and stealthy trying to sneak up to the cupboard and snatch a chocolate bar. You can become the loving parent who says "You know that chocolate bar is not good for you. Here's an apple." The chocolate bar, of course, being the old coping strategy and the apple is your new healthier choice.

One of my personal coping strategies for when I feel unsafe in the world is to become an uber-control freak. I become bossy and domineering and I attempt to take control of all the people around me. I feel like if I take control then I will be safe. Clearly, this is not an effective strategy. Now when I start to notice that I am becoming controlling or the loving people in my life kindly point it out I can laugh and say to my coping strategy "Kudos to you coping strategy. Nicely played, but no, I am not choosing to accept this negative coping strategy. Here is your apple."

Inner Child

Our inner child is the part of us that wants to play, have yummy food, go on adventures; it wants to have fun, creative, passionate experiences. But for many reasons we put aside our inner child. It could be trauma, it could be fear or it could be someone simply told us it wasn't ok anymore.

Our inner child is incredibly important to psychological well being. It contributes to our ability to find balance and happiness in our lives. I challenge you to really connect to your inner child. When that tiny voice inside your head says, go ahead and jump in that puddle or sing out loud or colour, dance, skip, play, cuddle, blow bubbles, make banana splits, have a tea party, take a moment and listen. Take a chance even if it is just a tiny little step. Play a game with your kids. Bum Wiggle!

I promise you, you will feel liberated, free. You will feel joy and happiness and isn't that what life is supposed to be about?

Patterns

You can recognize patterns when you are responding to certain events or emotions in exactly the same way every time. When you find yourself asking "Why am I doing this again?" or "Why do I end up in this same situation over and over?" and even when you can see the event taking place you cannot seem to change the course of action; kind of like watching a train wreck and feeling helpless to stop it. Chances are you are following a preset pattern, a pathway in your brain that goes into autopilot. Let me see if I can illustrate. Imagine a woman who is disappointed her partner did not bring home flowers for her birthday. She starts to validate her core belief that she is not loveable with stories like, "I'm not important," "He doesn't love me anymore" and she chooses to leave him. This is her 5th break up in a year. I used flowers as the catalyst in this example but any number of events could trigger the same pattern and the outcome is always the same.

When you become aware of a pattern the key is to take a deep breath and try something different. This is a great opportunity for Stop! Drop! & Wiggle!

Trauma

Trauma can have many sources and varying degrees of severity but the bottom line is that whether it is extreme or mild it has affected you in a profound way. It is not helpful to compare your trauma to other people's experiences; we all respond differently to different things. Also don't try to devalue or dismiss your experience because you think on some grand scale it's not worthy. Alternately, don't give it the power to force you to relive it over and over. It's important to acknowledge that it happened and that it sucked and it has had an influence on who you are today but it is not going to control who you are tomorrow.

If you have been hiding or denying your trauma don't be afraid to seek help. Reach out to a coach or therapist.

Many negative coping strategies are created as a survival method during trauma. If we can recognize these coping strategies and where they came from it becomes easier to let them go and replace them with healthier choices.

No matter what trauma you've experienced you have the power and the ability to make the shift from being the emotional victim who is reactive to the world around you to becoming someone who moves beyond the trauma and chooses to respond to the world by living a life of happiness and joy.

Triggers

A trigger is an event, sight, taste, sound or action that causes an emotional and physiological response. Triggers are created from intense emotional experiences and they can be either positive or negative. During these experiences our bodies, brain and senses take a snap shot of the moment capturing sights, sounds, words, environment, emotions and activities that were present at that time. When something in our present reminds us, even in the smallest way, of that moment it can become a trigger that takes you back in time to that moment.

To help illustrate consider a song from your past and you heard it for the very first time while on a date with someone you were head-over-heels in love with. Now every time you hear the song you are transported back to that first date. Or maybe you remember the smell of your campfire from the very first time you went camping and now whenever you smell a log fire you think back to your camping experience. These are our more common types of triggers and positive triggers are great; they bring back all sorts of wonderful memories. However, negative triggers can range from uncomfortable to down right terrifying and a trigger can be the tiniest sensory input like a word or a smell, or a sound so small that you might not even notice it and then suddenly you are transported back to a terrible moment in your life. And your brain may only choose to remember certain parts of the precipitating event so you may find yourself feeling anger or fear for no understandable reason or maybe you start to cry or you suddenly have an unexplained pain; there are unlimited possibilities.

If we can start to recognize when we are being triggered (for example; maybe your partner uses a word or phrase that always seems to make you more upset) we can start to learn to respond to them in different ways. Awareness gives us the opportunity to choose a different response.

An Emotional Check In can be helpful in these moments. Do a Check In and then ask yourself if what you are feeling could be attached to something in your past.

For deeper, more traumatic triggers, where you are transported back in time and cannot escape the intense emotional reaction try this "I Am in the Present Exercise."

I Am in the Present Exercise

This is how you practice the I am in the Present Exercise by yourself:

- Say to yourself out loud "I am triggered. This is not real. I want to come back into the present."

- Now list 5 items you see in the room.

- Now list 4 different items you see in the room.

- Now list 3 different items.

- Now 2.

- Now 1.

- Take a deep breath. If you are still not in the present start over at 5 new items and repeat until you are calm and back in the present.

This is how you can practice the I am in the Present Exercise with someone else:

- If you have a partner supporting you, you can teach them the above exercise and have them ask you to list the items as outlined above.

Biochemicals

Here are some of the biochemicals that are released in your body when you are feeling unpleasant emotions. Remember that in short doses it is normal and our bodies can handle it but in long or sustained output they can cause both long and short term physical and psychology illness.

Cortisol

Cortisol, also called hydrocortisone, an organic compound belonging to the steroid family that is the principal hormone secreted by the adrenal glands. It is a potent anti-inflammatory agent and is used for the palliative treatment of diseases such as rheumatoid arthritis.

Cortisol is the major glucocorticoid in humans. It has two primary actions: it stimulates gluconeogenesis—the breakdown of protein and fat to provide metabolites that can be converted to glucose in the liver—and it activates antistress and anti-inflammatory pathways. It also has weak mineralocorticoid activity. Cortisol plays a major role in the body's response to stress. It helps to maintain blood glucose concentrations by increasing gluconeogenesis and by blocking the uptake of glucose into tissues other than the central nervous system. It also contributes to the maintenance of blood pressure by augmenting the constrictive effects of catecholamines on blood vessels. ("cortisol")

Adrenaline and Noradrenaline (epinephrine and norepinephrine)

The actions of epinephrine and norepinephrine are generally similar, although they differ from each other in certain of their effects. Norepinephrine constricts almost all blood vessels, while epinephrine causes constriction in many networks of minute blood vessels but dilates the blood vessels in the skeletal muscles and the liver. Both hormones increase the rate and force of contraction of the heart, thus increasing the output of blood from the heart and increasing the blood pressure. The hormones also have important metabolic actions. Epinephrine stimulates the breakdown of glycogen to glucose in the liver, which results in the raising of the level of blood sugar. Both hormones increase the level of circulating free fatty acids. The extra amounts of glucose and fatty acids can be used by the body as fuel in times of stress or danger where increased alertness or exertion is required. Epinephrine is sometimes called the emergency hormone because it is released during stress and its stimulatory effects fortify and prepare an animal for either "fight or flight." ("epinephrine and norepinephrine")

The Next set of biochemicals I would like to talk about are some of the ones that are released when you are feeling happy, relaxed and content. There are a number of ways to promote the production of these biochemicals which support health and well being in your life and your body; in Stop! Drop! & Wiggle! we focus on laughter but also included in the list are play, meditation and orgasm.

Dopamine

Dopamine is produced in quite a few areas of the brain, including the substantia nigra and the ventral tegmental area. Dopamine is also a neurohormone released by the hypothalamus. Its principle hormonal role is to inhibit the release of prolactin from the anterior lobe of the pituitary. Dopamine has important roles in behavior and cognition, voluntary movement, motivation, punishment and reward, sleep, mood, attention, working memory and learning. ("Neurotransmitters and their functions" January 07, 2011)

Serotonin

Serotonin is a monoamine neurotransmitter, usually found in the gastrointestinal tract, platelets and the central nervous system. This chemical is also known as the "happiness hormone", because it arouses feelings of pleasure and well-being. Low levels of serotonin are associated with increased carbohydrate cravings, depression, sleep deprivations and hypersensitivity to pain. ("Neurotransmitters and their functions" January 07, 2011)

Endorphins

Endorphins are produced by the pituitary gland and the hypothalamus in vertebrates during exercise, excitement, pain, consumption of spicy food, love and orgasm. Endorphins contribute to the feeling of well-being and act similarly to opiates. They are also known to reduce pain and anxiety. ("Neurotransmitters and their functions" January 07, 2011)

Appendix B

Emotions Chart

Here is the companion Emotions Chart for the exercise in Chapter 7. You can photo copy this page and post it up on your wall.

Absorbed	Adoration	Aggravated	Alarmed
Alienated	Amused	Anger	Annoyed
Anticipating	Anxious	Aroused	Attraction
Awkward	Bitter	Bitter	Bored
Brave	Calm	Caring	Cautious
Cheerful	Comfortable	Compassionate	Concern
Confused	Confused	Contempt	Content
Curious	Defeated	Delight	Depressed
Disappointed	Disgraced	Disgusted	Disillusioned
Dislike	Disoriented	Distrust	Disturbed
Dread	Eager	Elated	Embarrassed
Enthusiastic	Exasperated	Excited	Exhausted
Exhilarated	Fear	Fondness	Frustrated
Grief	Grief-stricken	Grumpy	Guilty
Happy	Hateful	Helpless	Hesitant
Hope	Hopeful	Hopeless	Horrified
Hostile	Humiliated	Humiliated	Hurt
Hurt	Indifferent	Infatuated	Inferior
Insecure	Insulted	Interest	Interested
Intrigued	Irritated	Isolated	Jealous
Joyful	Liked	Lonely	Love
Lust	Melancholy	Neglected	Nervous
Numb	Optimistic	Outrage	Overwhelmed
Panic	Pity	Pleased	Powerless
Preoccupied	Proud	Rage	Receptive
Regret	Rejected	Relaxed	Resentful
Restless	Sad	Safe	Satisfied
Scared	Scornful	Self conscious	Shame
Shocked	Sorrow	Spiteful	Stressed
Suspicious	Sympathy	Tenderness	Terror
Trust	Trusting	Uncertain	Uncomfortable
Vengeful	Weary	Worried	

References

Encyclopædia Britannica Online, s. v. "**cortisol**," accessed February 13, 2014, http://www.britannica.com/EBchecked/topic/138929/cortisol.

Encyclopædia Britannica Online, s. v. "**epinephrine and norepinephrine**," accessed February 13, 2014, http://www.britannica.com/EBchecked/topic/190049/epinephrine.

SteadyHealth.com, "**Neurotransmitters and their functions.**" Last modified January 07, 2011. Accessed February 13, 2014. http://ic.steadyhealth.com/neurotransmitters_and_their_functions.html.

Resources

Succulent Living: You can reach out to **Gaia Morrissette** for coaching and support. It is also where to find Stop! Drop! & Wiggle! supporting products and events. www.succulentliving.com

Feel the Fear and Do It Anyway® by Susan Jeffers, Ph.D: You can find this life changing book on www.succulentliving.com if you want to learn about workshops and other events please visit www.susanjeffers.com

Abounding River Board Game: Created by www.cafegratitude.com http://cafegratitude.com/store/shop/books-dvds/abounding-river-board-game-version-two-smaller-size/

Theta Brain Wave Audio Mediation: Created by Brain sync which can be found on www.succulentliving.com

Sarah Morrissette: Owner of Peace Alive. She is an amazing and gifted Energy therapist that specializes in Reiki, EFT, BEAM therapies. Visit her at www.peacealive.com

Pierre Black: Montreal based Naturotherapist specializing in Chinese, Ayurvedic and Naturopathic medicines. He has been important part of my health and wellness team. He will change your life not just your health. http://pierreblack.com/

AL Link and Pala Copeland: Owners, teachers and authors at 4 Freedoms Relationship Tantra. They are my mentors and now my dear colleagues. Please visit them at www.tantra-sex.com

Maryam M: Graphic Designer, Artist and Illustrator. The cute graphic of me throughout the book was created by her. I highly recommend her. scorpio1576@gmail.com

Supplementary Reading

Gerasimo, Pilar. Experience Life, **"Emotional Biochemistry."** Last modified December 2003. Accessed February 21, 2014. http://experiencelife.com/article/emotional-biochemistry/.

Najemy, Robert Elias. SelfGrowth.com, **"The Chemistry of Emotions."** Last modified February 13, 2008. Accessed February 21, 2014. http://www.selfgrowth.com/articles/The_Chemistry_Of_Emotions.html.

Puder, Christine. **"The healthful effects of laughter."** *Journal of Child and Youth Care.* (1998): 45-53. http://www.cyc-net.org/cyc-online/cycol-0803-humour.html (accessed February 21, 2014).

Robinson, Joe. The Huffington Post, **"The Key to Happiness: A Taboo for Adults?."** Last modified January 18, 2011. Accessed February 21, 2014. http://www.huffingtonpost.com/joe-robinson/why-is-the-key-source-of-_b_809719.html.

Letter from the Author

Dear Reader,

Thank you from the bottom of my heart for going on this adventure with me. Sharing Stop! Drop! & Wiggle! and all the other tools and knowledge contained in this book has been an incredible journey of learning, self discovery and delightful bum wiggling for me.

I am now looking forward to being able to interact with you and to hear all about your amazing and happy new life! Let me know how Stop! Drop! & Wiggle! has affected your life. You can send your life changing stories or love notes to gaia@succulentliving.com.

I'd also like to invite you to participate in my Laugh Tracks project. They say that laughter is contagious and I absolutely believe this to be true. I am seeking volunteers to provide me their best and funniest laugh tracks to create a series of compilation CDs which I believe will be a great way to help people laugh more. So if you are interested in participating in this project you can contact me gaia@succulentliving.com for details.

If you are seeking personal one-on-one support for healing or you need help sorting through old core beliefs and coping strategies or you just need a fellow cheerleader of happiness to hold your hand while you are making changes in your life please contact me at gaia@succulentliving. com to inquire about my professional coaching services.

Author Bio

Gaia Morrissette, has dedicated her life to making the world a happier, sexier and safer place for us all. She is a world renowned Sexual Wellness Coach, Author, Columnist, Happiness Specialist, Pottery & Drumming Teacher, Artist and founder of Succulent Living. Through her Sexual Wellness Coaching Private Practice; she makes sex safe, makes sex better and helps you take it to next level. Her philosophy is that for true sexual wellness to happen you must look at these 5 aspects: Play, Sensuality, Sexuality, Exploration and Sacred. **Stop, Drop and Wiggle!** explores the first aspect which is our foundation of Happiness: PLAY.

Her education and training consist of, sexology, trauma recovery, life coaching, tantra training, sex coaching, and lots of practice in the areas of play, healing, and exploring.

Some of Gaia's passions that support her incredible life are: exploring the world's natural wonders, sitting quietly mediating by an ocean, climbing trees in the jungles with the monkeys, frolicking in the sea with the dolphins and dancing on the beach in the full moon light. Her soul and creativity soars when she is with Mother Nature. When Gaia is not travelling and frolicking in nature she enjoys spending time chilling out with her awesome husband and lively dog Zeus in South western Ontario, Canada or playing drums in the park. For more information about Gaia and her professional practice, please visit www.succulentliving.com.